A Splash of Spring

by
Susanne Glover
and
Georgeann Grewe

illustrated by Georgeann Grewe

Cover by Vanessa Filkins

Copyright © Good Apple, Inc., 1987

ISBN No. 0-86653-412-1

Printing No. 9876543

GOOD APPLE, INC.
BOX 299
CARTHAGE, ILLINOIS 62321-0299

Dedicated to:
my cousin ANNETTE

TABLE OF CONTENTS

TEACHER TIPS

WELCOME, SPRING (page 1)

* Make this wreath a monthly decoration by using the patterns included for March, April and May. Add patterns of your own for variety.

WELCOME, SPRING (pages 1-17)

* Introduce spring or culminate a study of spring by presenting a program for other children. Choose activities from those provided and/or supplement with those ideas of your own. Adapt the material to your grade level.

A FINE FLOCK (pages 18-37)

* Establish the mood in your classroom for this unit by developing the bulletin board and by building a small library using materials you have available.
* Prepare an all-day or all-week unit of study of birds by combining the various activities found in this section which are appropriate to your grade level.
* Attach learning packets to the birds on the bulletin board to create a center for study. Use the materials prepared in this unit as well as your own.

STATIONERY (pages 32, 40, 60, 67, 78, 99)

* Give children this form to write home about their progress.
* Assign work to be completed on this paper to use as a display on a bulletin board or for something special.

COPYCAT (pages 42, 71, 120)

* Read and discuss the poem orally with the class, discussing format, rhyme, capital letters and punctuation before assigning children to copy the poem in their best writing.

FINE FEATHERED FRIENDS (page 27)

* Have children copy the information. Then attach to the bulletin board to display penmanship.

BIRD OBSERVATION RECORD (page 28)

* Use this ditto for interested individuals or for an entire class project. Take time to discuss those birds observed with your students.

FLY THE COOP (pages 29, 30)

* Although this game was designed with spelling in mind, the blank cards provided make it a most versatile gameboard. Use it as a trivia game prepared by students in your class, reviewing subject or several content areas.

LAMB WORK SHEETS (pages 40, 41)

* Use the large lamb as a handwriting page for creative writing to use in conjunction with the ewe door knocker.
* Create a game using the large lamb either for directions or a gameboard. Use the smaller sheep for game pieces or for a related activity.

FASHION FACTORY (pages 43-80)

* Prepare this unit of study for Easter or spring by choosing appropriate activities for your students and teaching those necessary lessons so that children can proceed independently after all directions are given. This section is complete with a report card for easy evaluation

as well as a certificate for students completing work provided. Activities may be introduced daily and packets of work made available on the bulletin board, or you may wish to do only a few lessons each week. Advanced students may be able to pursue activities with little guidance. However, all students should be aware of the lessons available, procedures, and your evaluation system before the unit begins! Slight teacher preparation will be necessary.

* Substitute or add your own lessons to create a well-rounded program of learning.
* Display completed projects throughout the room to create a warm, busy, learning mood.
* Find several books appropriate to your grade and interest level to encourage students to read books for their book reports.

SCRAMBLED EGGS (pages 51, 52)

* Although this lesson was developed for spelling, adapt it to fit any content area. Examples: Math Match, Vocabulary Match, etc.

STRICTLY BUSINESS (pages 59-62)

* Teach children how to correctly write a business letter by having them study the letter in this section. Use the blank form to allow students to practice writing a business letter. The addresses which follow in this section are provided so that children can write for free/inexpensive materials of their choice. You may need to teach envelope addressing and/or how to write a postcard.

FACTS/A TALE TO TELL (pages 66, 67)

* Have students add details to the Facts page and then incorporate these facts and details into a story on the following page.

A HARE RACING EVENT (pages 74-77)

* After Xeroxing the game cards, the teacher should write the capital for each state on the back. On the others, write the state where each important place is found.

WE'RE GROWING (page 81-85)

* Use the bulletin board for a variety of concepts. We have suggested ADJECTIVES. However, most concepts could be substituted.

ANTICIPATION (pages 88-99)

* Extend the bulletin board theme to include an all-day or week-long study of ants. Begin by creating the bulletin board to display in the classroom. Then incorporate all of the content areas included in this section supplemented with ideas of your own. Choose lessons suitable for your grade level or adapt them to suit your needs. Perhaps select a book about ants for your focus of teaching material. Then follow up with the activities provided in this section.

FOOTLOOSE (pages 100-117)

* Use the bulletin board and extended activities to motivate children the last few weeks or days of school. Begin with the development of the bulletin board, allowing each student to create his part of the worm, complete with a writing activity or other suggested ideas. Take time to enjoy your students as you complete the activities together.
* Motivate your students to explore the arts as they try "Toe"l Painting, Shoe Designing, and Footprinting.
* Allow time for individuals to make a Footloose booklet and finish the activities suggested. (Challenge students to add additional pages of their own to the Footloose booklet.)

COME SPRING

SPLASH ME YELLOW! SPLASH ME
    GREEN!
THESE TINY BUDS NOW CAN BE SEEN—
    TULIPS, CROCUSES, DAFFODILS,
A RED-BREASTED ROBIN ON MY WINDOW—
    SILL!
SUNLIGHT WARMING THE CRISP SPRING
    AIR,
SIGNS OF NEW LIFE EVERYWHERE.
A BURST OF ENERGY, JUST TAKE A
    LOOK—
THERE'S FUN FOR KIDS INSIDE THIS
    BOOK!

Welcome, Spring

TO CREATE THE BULLETIN BOARD, YOU WILL NEED:
1. A large sheet of white or light-green background paper.
2. Patterns for the letters in the title which can be found on the following pages.
3. Dark-green and pale-pink construction paper for the shamrock patterns which follow.
4. A large white or pink bow for the wreath, either real for 3-D effect or a flat paper bow. A calico bow would also be attractive.

PRACTICAL USES:
1. Write the name of each student in your class on a shamrock. Use the bulletin board to display students in your class.
2. Attach a school picture to the child's shamrock pattern.
3. Give each student a shamrock pattern. Ask him to write THREE WISHES, one on each section of the shamrock. Or have student describe a LUCKY experience.
*4. Use the April and May patterns in this section to create a classroom wreath for the spring season. Change the bulletin board title to "Welcome, April" or "Welcome, May."

4

BLOOMINGVALES

Multiply each fact and write your answer in the center of each flower. When you finish, color all even numbered answers red and all odd numbered answers yellow. Add a green stem to each flower.

PROGRAM IDEAS

Whether it is used as a culminating activity for the study of birds or as an introduction to the season of spring, this program is sure to delight not only your students but fellow students and parents as well. Here are a few ideas you may want to try with your class.

1. SPRING

    Get six large sturdy pieces of cardboard, preferably white. Print one letter of the word *spring* on each card. On the back of each card, paste the corresponding couplet for that letter, which can be found on page 11. Choose six students to introduce the program by standing on stage with their letter posters facing away from the audience. The student holding poster S will turn his poster around and say his couplet. Poster P will do the same, and so on. When all six children have recited their couplets, the posters will spell the word *spring* . You may wish children to dress representative of the meanings of their couplets.

2. MUSIC

    To add variety before, during, and/or after the program, use the music suggested on page 9 or songs of your choice. (Let students play instruments, sing, or use a record player or tape for assistance if necessary.)

3. THIS IS THE NEST THAT ROBIN BUILT

    Modeled after the Mother Goose rhyme, this story can be told very simply or with lots of props and fun. To involve several children, let children dress up or make props to fit the story lines, with a different student (11 total) for each segment of the story. A large nest on the stage would be darling. Puppetry is also another approach.

4. JUST ME

    This choral reading can involve your entire class. Select students to memorize or recite various parts. Add costumes and a touch of scenery, or make this a simple reading.

5. SETTING THE STAGE

    To create a mood for your program, display bird posters and projects around the viewing area. If the program is an introduction to spring, you may wish a simple backdrop of a spring scene! Be creative. Let students get involved in the decision making.

WELCOME, SPRING

Look over the ideas presented on the previous pages. Think of the talents and abilities of the students in your class. Combine the activities provided with those of your own to capture a well-rounded presentation for spring. Share this program with other children in the school. Remember the parents! Once you have selected the activities you want in the program, write them in program form on your chalkboard in neat print. Give each student a copy of the program cover found on page 10. Have him copy the program neatly inside and then color the cover. Give completed programs to teachers, parents, and others attending.

Here is a suggested program itinerary.
  I. Parade of the Students (7—announcer + 6 for SPRING)

 II. Welcome

III. Spring

 IV. Song

  V. This Is the Nest That Robin Built

 VI. Song

VII. Choral Reading (Just Me)

VIII. Song (May invite audience to join in singing as children parade from the room.)

Musical Resources:
A. Silver Burdett Co. MUSIC (Centennial Edition)
    1. The Barnyard
    2. The Tree in the Wood
    3. Rain, Rain Go Away
    4. Sing a Rainbow
    5. Springtime (La Primavera)

B. Holt, Rinehart, & Winston. EXPLORING MUSIC
    1. The Coming of Spring
    2. Spring Song

Program cover

is for SUNSHINE to brighten the spring,
Warming the water, the earth, everything!

 is for POSIES with colors so bright—
Reds, yellows, purples, Oh! what a sight!

 is for RAINDROPS that splash all about,
Wetting the earth so that new life can sprout.

 is for INSECTS that flit through the air,
And the grasshoppers, beetles, and ants everywhere.

 is for NOISES I hear when I wake,
The chirping of birds and the laughs children make.

is for GROWTH that I see around me.
The plants and the animals—SPRING is lovely!

This Is the Nest That Robin Built

This is the nest that Robin built.

This is the egg that lay in the nest
    that Robin built.

This is the shell that came from the egg
    that lay in the nest
    that Robin built.

This is the peep that hatched from the shell
    that once held the egg
    that lay in the nest
    that Robin built.

This is the worm that fed the peep
    that hatched from the shell
    that once held the egg
    that lay in the nest
    that Robin built.

This is the mama with feathered wings
    that found the worm that fed the peep
    that hatched from the shell
    that once held the egg
    that lay in the nest
    that Robin built.

This is the song the robin sings
    to her pretty mama with feathered wings
    when she found the worm that fed the peep
    that hatched from the shell
    that once held the egg
    that lay in the nest
    that Robin built.

This is the cat that knows all things
     that heard the song the robin sings
     to her pretty mama with feathered wings
     when she found the worm that fed the peep
     that hatched from the shell
     that once held the egg
     that lay in the nest
     that Robin built.

This is the dog that likes everything
     that chased the cat that knows all things
     that heard the song the robin sings
     to her pretty mama with feathered wings
     when she found the worm that fed the peep
     that hatched from the shell
     that once held the egg
     that lay in the nest
     that Robin built.

This is the sun that shines in Spring
     that wakes the dog that likes everything
     that chased the cat that knows all things
     that heard the song the robin sings
     to her pretty mama with feathered wings
     when she found the worm that fed the peep
     that hatched from the shell
     that once held the egg
     that lay in the nest
     that Robin built.

This is the tree that the robin's nest clings
     that is warmed by the sun that shines in Spring
     that wakes the dog that likes everything
     that chased the cat that knows all things
     that heard the song the robin sings
     to her pretty mama with feathered wings
     when she found the worm that fed the peep
     that hatched from the shell
     that once held the egg
     that lay in the nest
     that Robin built.

JUST ME

DUCKS:

We are fat, yellow ducks
With feathers on our backs.
We wish we could talk,
But we just say "QUACK."
We waddle to the pond
On our two webbed feet.
We have a long, flat bill
To catch the bugs that we eat.
We're so close to the ground
That we'll never grow up.
We wish that we could be
Little beagle pups!

PUPPIES:

(Make barking sounds . . . arf, arf, arf, arf)
We are newborn puppies
With teeth that bite.
Our bellies are brown
And black and white.
Our ears hang low;
Long tails we wag.
We chew on shoes
Instead of old rags.
We gnaw old bones
From folks so nice.
But we'd like to be tiny
As little gray mice.

MICE:

(Make squeaking sounds . . . squeak, squeak, squeak)
We are little gray mice
With great big ears,
And we scurry about
Raising people's fears.
They set out traps
With fresh, yellow cheese,
Just hoping to catch
Us all, you see!
We'd like to be friendly
But we don't know how.
It would be a lot simpler
If we could be cows!

14

COWS:

(Make mooing sounds—moo, moo, moo)
Out in green fields
We stand all day,
Swishing our long tails
And munching on hay.
Around our heads
Buzz lots of flies—
Landing in our ears
And our big, brown eyes.
Many buckets we fill up
With milk to drink.
It would be much more fun
To be snakes, we think!

SNAKES:

(Make hissing sounds . . . sssss, sssss, sssss)
In the tall, waving grass
We slither and slide,
Then we quickly dart into
A deep hole to hide.
We have no legs
Nor teeth for prey;
Instead our fangs
Kill food for today.
We'd like to be able
To fly in the air
Like a sparrow or robin—
We really don't care!

BIRDS:

(Make chirping sounds . . . chirp, chirp, chirp)
We dart so swiftly
From tree to earth,
Searching for worms
For our babies' births.
Our nests are well-hidden
High up in trees.
Tiny blue eggshells
Bring fond memories.
Our wings must keep moving
Flying sure wears us out.
To go slowly as a turtle
Would be great, no doubt!

TURTLES:

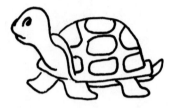

(Make no noise . . . silence;
scoot into view via skateboards or dollies)
With our house on our back
And our tails tucked inside,
We pull in our head, arms
And legs to hide.
We look like a rock
And we don't make a sound.
Then we slowly move on
When no one's around.
We creep right along.
Cause, GEE, what's the hurry—
We don't get much attention
Because we're not furry!

SKUNKS:

(Make spraying sounds)
With our shiny, black coat
And our pretty white stripe,
We think that we make
Such a beautiful sight.
We don't have many friends
But we really don't care—
We've got a scent
That will surely fill the air!
But the people get mad
And run, of course,
So just for once we'd
Like to be a horse!

HORSES:

(Make neighing sounds)
Sleek, chestnut horses
Now chomping on hay or
Running free in a field
On a bright, sunny day.
We have four hooves
And wear horseshoes.
We carry young children
Wherever they choose.
But then we're tired,
Our feet sore, you see—
We'd rather be ANYONE
But NOT JUST ME!

ALL:
Now we all are unhappy,
We'd much rather be
Someone much different
Than little OLE ME!

DUCKS:
But we can swim!

PUPPIES:
And we can bark!

MICE:
And we scare people
In daytime or dark!

COWS:
And we give milk!

SNAKES:
We keep away pests!

BIRDS:
And we fill up
Your trees with nests!

TURTLES:
And we show patience!

SKUNKS:
We perfume the air!

HORSES:
And we're fun to ride
Almost anywhere!

ALL:
So you can imagine,
And you can guess
That we're the ones
Who started this mess
Of wanting to be
Someone else, you see—
So we think we'd rather
Just keep being ME!

TO CREATE THE BULLETIN BOARD, YOU WILL NEED:

1. A large sheet of light-blue background paper.
2. Patterns for the letters in the title which can be found on the following pages.
3. White clouds made from a large sheet of white poster paper.
4. A copy of the rebus bird puzzle or the paragraph about birds for the display.
5. Patterns and oaktag or construction paper to make the birds onto which the assignment is attached.

PRACTICAL USES:

1. Use the bulletin board to display projects and/or reports about birds.
2. Attach good work to the birds to display on the bulletin board.
3. Place a learning packet on each bird and use the bulletin board as an activity station.

19

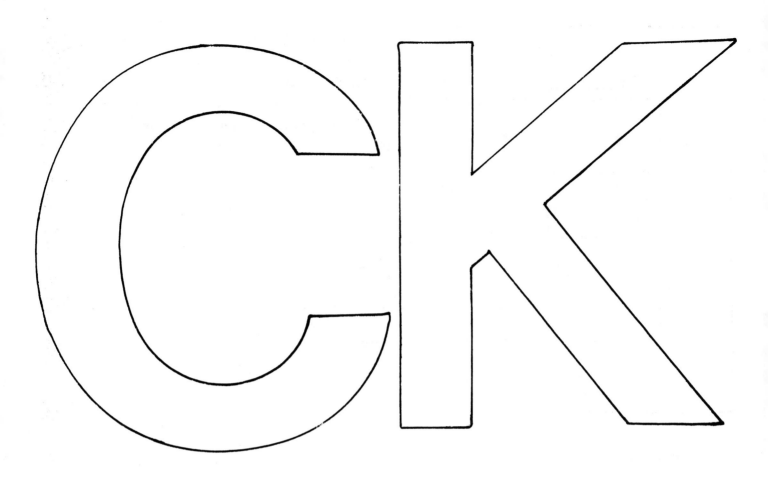

To complete this project you will need a head, right and left wing, and the feet. After you complete the writing activity, attach the above mentioned parts of the bird to your paper. Give it to your teacher to display on the bulletin board.

Feet

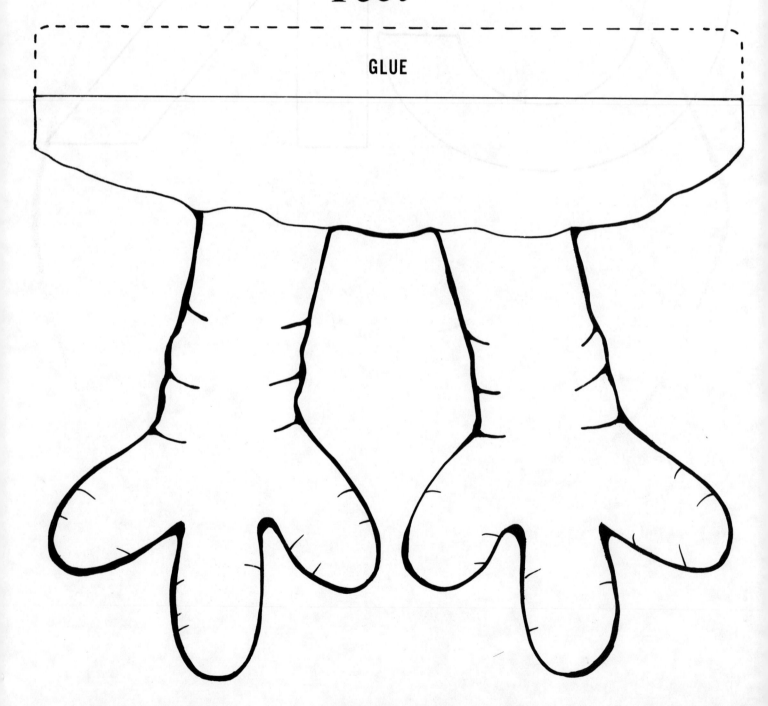

GLUE

Head

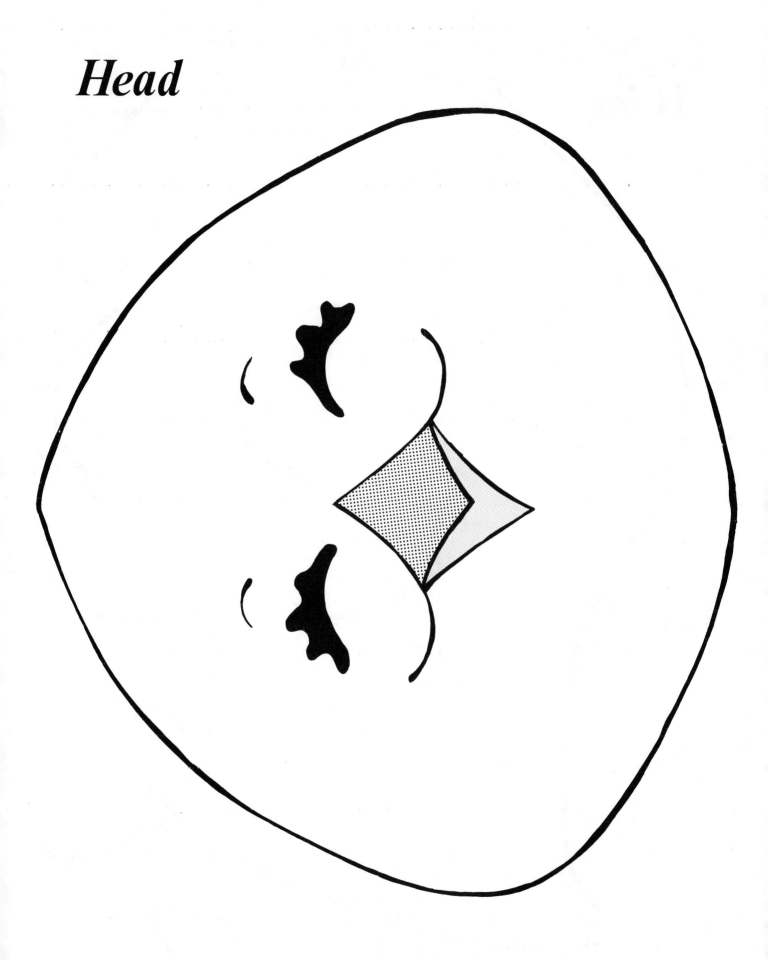

23

Left Wing

GLUE

GLUE

Right
Wing

LING

2 +

Fine Feathered Friends

Some birds are a brilliant color. Some birds cannot fly. Birds may vary greatly in size and shape. Even though birds can have striking differences, there are three things that are true of all birds of the world. First, all birds have feathers. Second, all birds hatch from eggs. And third, all birds have two legs.

_____

_____

_____

_____

_____

_____

_____

_____

_____

_____

_____

_____

_____

_____

_____

_____

_____

_____

_____

_____

_____

_____

Bird Observation Record

COLOR	SIZE	SHAPE feet, head, beak	SONG or call	FOOD	NEST type/location	EGGS

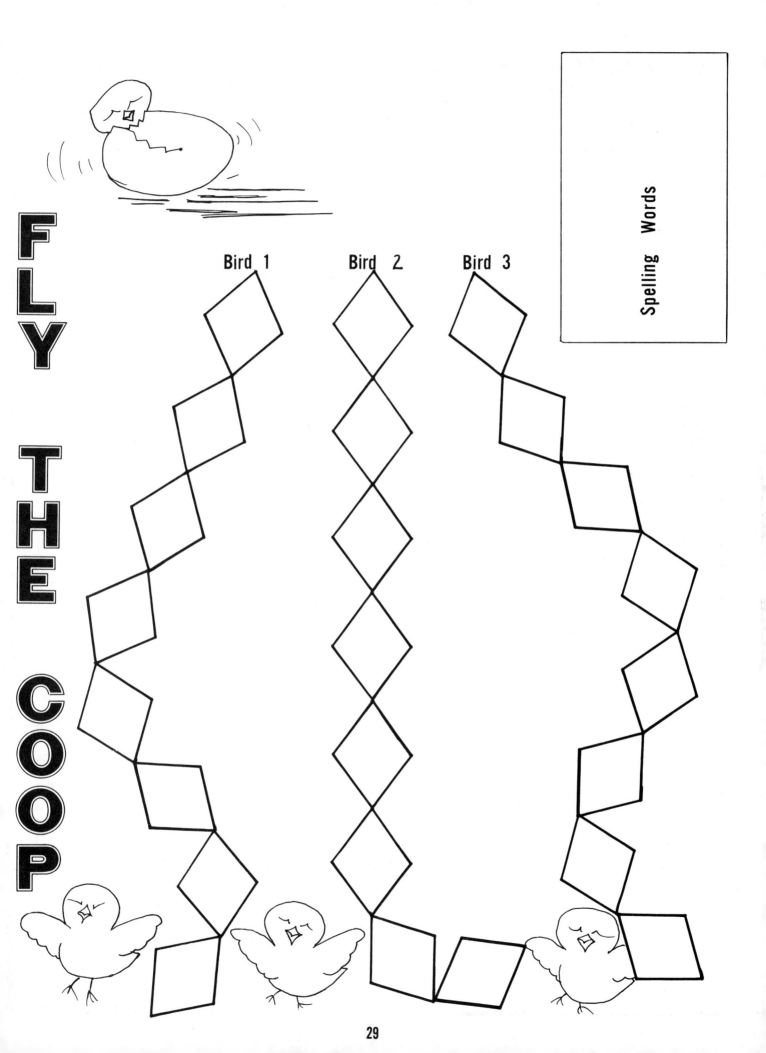

FLY THE COOP

Bird 1   Bird 2   Bird 3

Spelling Words

FLY THE COOP game cards are quite versatile. One suggestion is to have students write their spelling words for the week on one side and on the reverse, write the definitions. The three players take turns asking either the definition or the spelling of a word. Correct responses allow the player to move ahead one space. For incorrect answers, a player remains where he is. A second suggestion is to use the cards for the Bird Brains trivia questions which students create from research. Other gameboard possibilities include math facts or reading vocabulary.

Plot:

Title:

Author:

Setting:

Characters:

BOOK REPORT

by:

Best Part:

BIRD BRAINS

Use the code below to find the value of each BIRD. Circle the bird with the greatest value in each row.

A 1	B 2	C 3	D 4	E 5	F 6	G 7	H 8
I 9	J 10	K 11	L 12	M 13	N 14	O 15	P 16
Q 17	R 18	S 19	T 20	U 21	V 22	W 23	X 24
Y 25	Z 26						

E ___
Eagle

G ___
Goose

R ___
Robin

Q ___
Quail

S ___
Snipe

S ___
Sparrow

P ___
Peacock

B ___
Bittern

P ___
Pelican

W ___
Warbler

T ___
Turkey

M ___
Magpie

C ___
Cuckoo

T ___
Toucan

P ___
Parrot

33

COME FLY WITH ME
SCIENCE

The activities in this science activity packet may be done individually, in small groups, or as a class. The variety is sure to capture the attention of your students. Get a sturdy envelope. Cut out both the picture and the title strip on this page and glue them to the envelope. Cut out the eggs on the following pages and place them inside the envelope. Place the envelope in a strategic place in the classroom so that all students will have access. Allow children to submit their own science activities. Display completed activities in your classroom or throughout the school.

1. Ask a local sportsman or sports store to provide stuffed birds to display in your classroom.

2. Build a birdhouse. Hang it near a window by your classroom.

3. Research your state bird and tell your class about your findings. Include a colored drawing of it.

4. Bring an empty bird nest to school. Try to find out what kind of bird lived in the nest. (The location where you found it may help determine the species.)

5. Bring some fertilized eggs to put in your classroom incubator. Properly care for them with the help of an adult until they hatch.

6. Invite someone who raises chickens to be a guest speaker for your class.

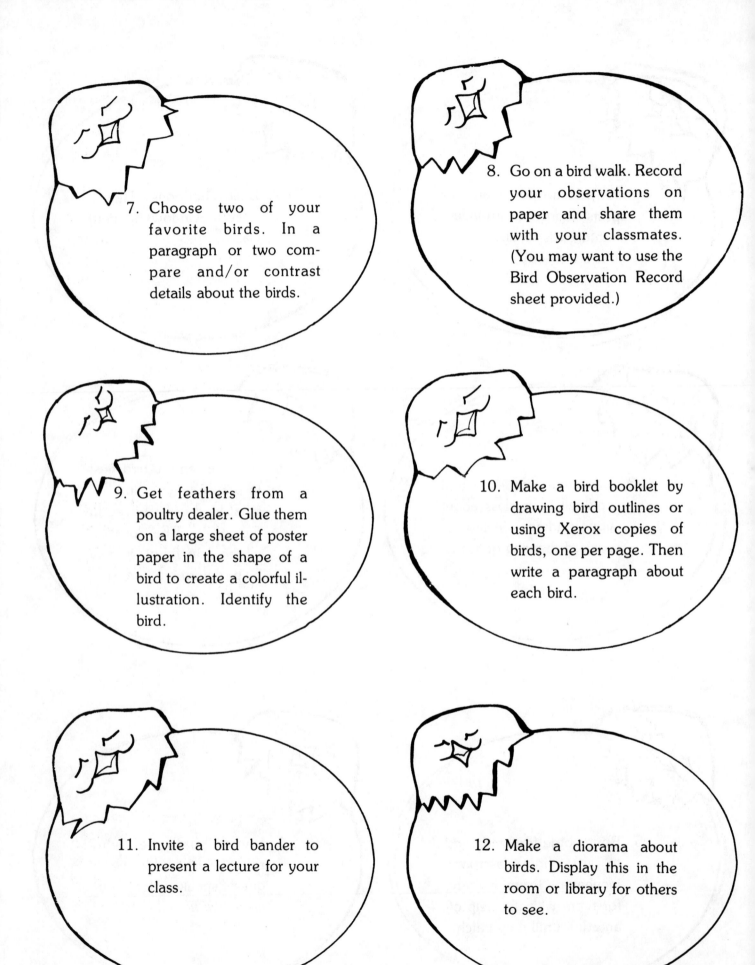

7. Choose two of your favorite birds. In a paragraph or two compare and/or contrast details about the birds.

8. Go on a bird walk. Record your observations on paper and share them with your classmates. (You may want to use the Bird Observation Record sheet provided.)

9. Get feathers from a poultry dealer. Glue them on a large sheet of poster paper in the shape of a bird to create a colorful illustration. Identify the bird.

10. Make a bird booklet by drawing bird outlines or using Xerox copies of birds, one per page. Then write a paragraph about each bird.

11. Invite a bird bander to present a lecture for your class.

12. Make a diorama about birds. Display this in the room or library for others to see.

13. Tape-record bird calls from live birds, bird callers, or from records. Share the recording with your class. Try to identify the calls.

14. Make a bird puzzle. Mount a large colored illustration of a bird onto sturdy cardboard. Label the bird type. Cut apart your picture carefully and place the puzzle pieces in an envelope. Share this fun with your friends.

15. Choose a friend or two and create a large mural about birds to hang in the hall or in your classroom.

16. Make bird flash cards from blank index cards. On one side glue a colored picture of a bird. On the other side, write the name of the bird.

17. Visit a bird sanctuary. Tell the class about your experience either by writing a report or by telling them.

18. Make up a crossword or a word hunt puzzle about birds. Ask your teacher to duplicate copies of it to distribute in the classroom.

DOOR KNOCKER

Your students will be delighted to see that the first sign of spring can be found on their classroom door. Title it "Ewe! It's Spring."

Give each student a copy of the art project/pattern found on the following page. Carefully explain the lesson so that each child can correctly make the lamb described. When all children have completed their project, display lambs on your classroom door.

EWE! A LAMB

MATERIALS:

1. small paper cup
2. cotton balls
3. glue
4. scissors
5. crayons or markers
6. lamb pattern

DIRECTIONS:

1. Color and cut out the lamb's head and legs.
2. Glue the head to the flat bottom of a small cup.
3. Fold the legs on the dotted lines. Glue them to the bottom of the cup.
4. Attach cotton balls (fluffed) to the sides of the cup and parts of the lamb.
5. Give your completed lamb to your teacher to display.

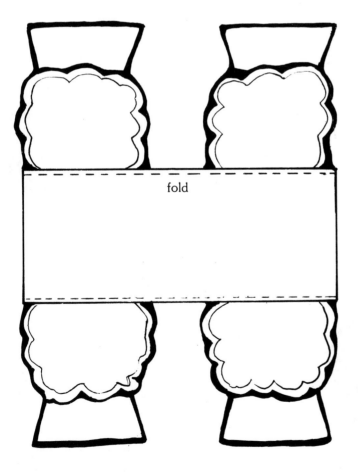

fold

COPYCAT

OOOOH! IT'S SPRING!

The trees are starting to sprout,
Little animals scurry about.
Oooooh! It's Spring,
I see everything
From daffodils to rainbow trout.

The sun is warming the air,
Raindrops fall everywhere.
Oooooh! It's Spring,
I feel everything
As the March winds blow through my hair.

Birds are chirping in their nest,
Children aren't stopping to rest.
Oooooh! It's Spring,
I hear everything
And I know I like this season best!

_____
_____
_____
_____
_____
_____
_____
_____
_____
_____
_____
_____

TO CREATE THE BULLETIN BOARD, YOU WILL NEED:

1. A large sheet of yellow background paper.
2. Patterns for the letters in the title which can be found on the following pages.
3. A large piece of white poster paper for the rabbit. Glue cotton balls onto the rabbit to create a furry effect for dimension.
4. Several large sheets of various colored poster paper for eggs onto which a variety of learning packets will be attached.

PRACTICAL USES:

1. Select several activities provided in this section to create "fun" learning for your students. Make several copies of the activities and place them into a learning packet (envelope), complete with directions. Place a few on different eggs attached to the bulletin board to develop a learning center. Change the packets as often as you feel necessary.
2. Use several eggs around the rabbit as a display area for good work. Change the title to "EGG"-cellent Work!
3. Display various completed projects on the bulletin board.

44

45

46

47

BOY

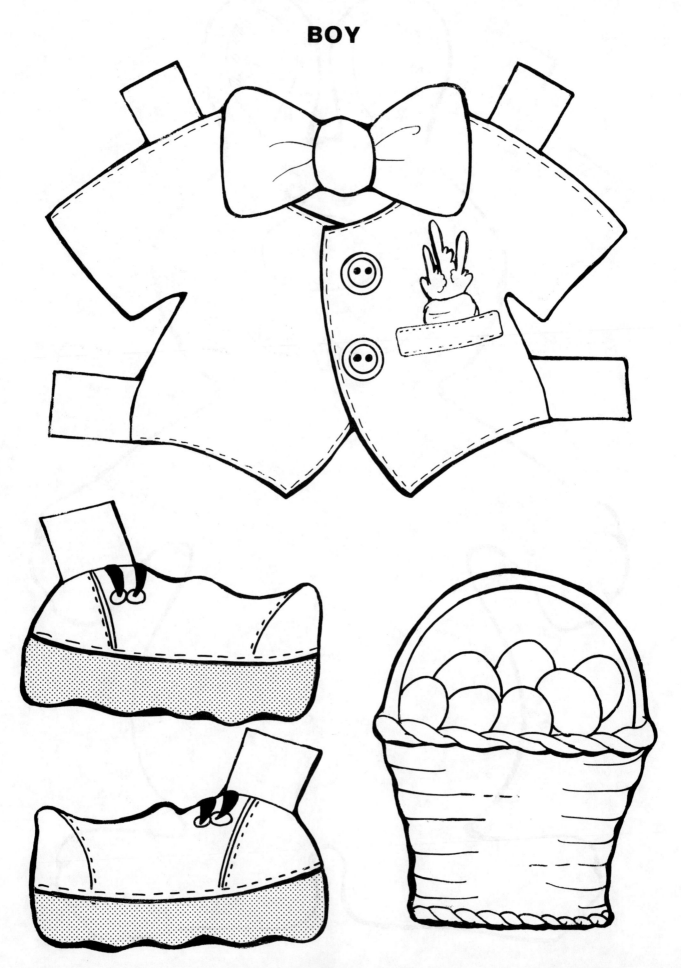

GIRL

QUACK-UPS

On the left side of this page you will find clues. The answers to the clues will be SYNONYMS that rhyme. Write the correct response in the blank.

1. Fat branch   _ _ _ _ _ _ _ O _ _

2. Semi chuckle   _ _ _ _ O _ _ _ _

3. Cryin' bird   _ O _ _ _ _ _ _ _ _

4. More intelligent hat   _ _ _ _ _ O _ _ _ _

5. Bitter rose   _ _ _ _ _ _ _ _ O _

6. Superior home for birds   _ _ O _ _ _ _ _

7. Downpour window   _ _ _ _ O _ _ _

8. Bunny custom   O _ _ _ _ _ _ _ _ _ _

9. Biting insect snack   _ _ _ _ O _ _ _ _ _ _

10. Thin bird   O _ _ _ _ _ _ _ _ _ _ _

11. Toad run   _ _ _ O _ _ _

12. Crooked shelter   _ _ _ _ _ _ _ O

13. Dandy evergreen   _ _ _ _ _ O _ _

14. Night crawler wiggle   _ _ _ O _ _ _ _ _ _

15. False reptile   _ _ _ _ _ _ _ O

Now write each letter found in the circles in the order in which they appear. This will be a message to you.

___ ___ ___ ___ ___ ___ ___ ___ ___ ___ .

50

SCRAMBLED EGGS

Cut out all of the eggs found on this page. Glue them to the matching eggs on the previous page. Now turn your paper over and write each word in a sentence. Be sure to spell them correctly! Use your best handwriting.

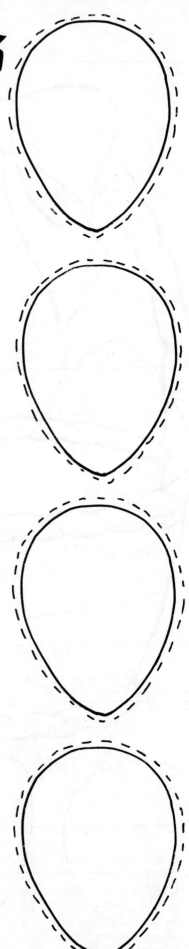
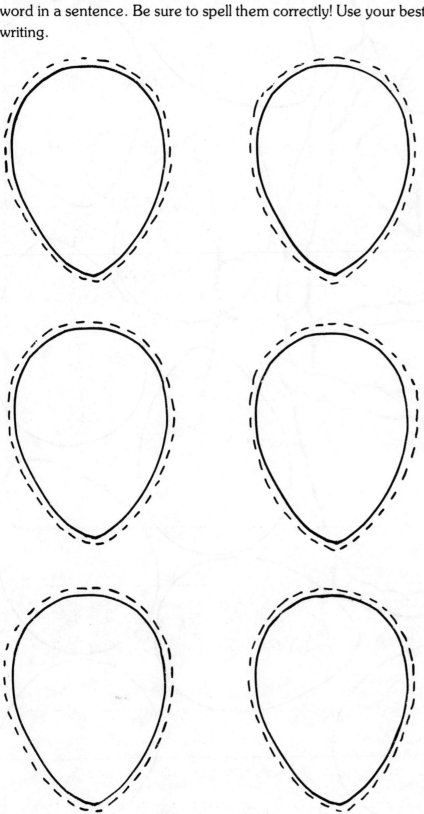

ABOUT ADVERBS

Language Arts

Individually or in groups of two, your students will find this activity most beneficial as well as enjoyable. Be sure to teach the concept of ADVERBS first. Then use this station as a review. Get a sturdy envelope. Cut out both the picture and the title strip on this page and glue them to the envelope. Cut apart all of the activity pieces on the following pages (rabbits, eggs, carrots, baskets). Place them inside the envelope. Now make several copies of the work sheet ADVERBS to place in a packet near the envelope. Have students complete the work sheet and then follow your directions. (HINT: To make the work sheet easy to grade, all of the sentences written on BASKETS = TIME; CARROTS = PLACE; EGGS = MANNER; RABBITS = DEGREE.)

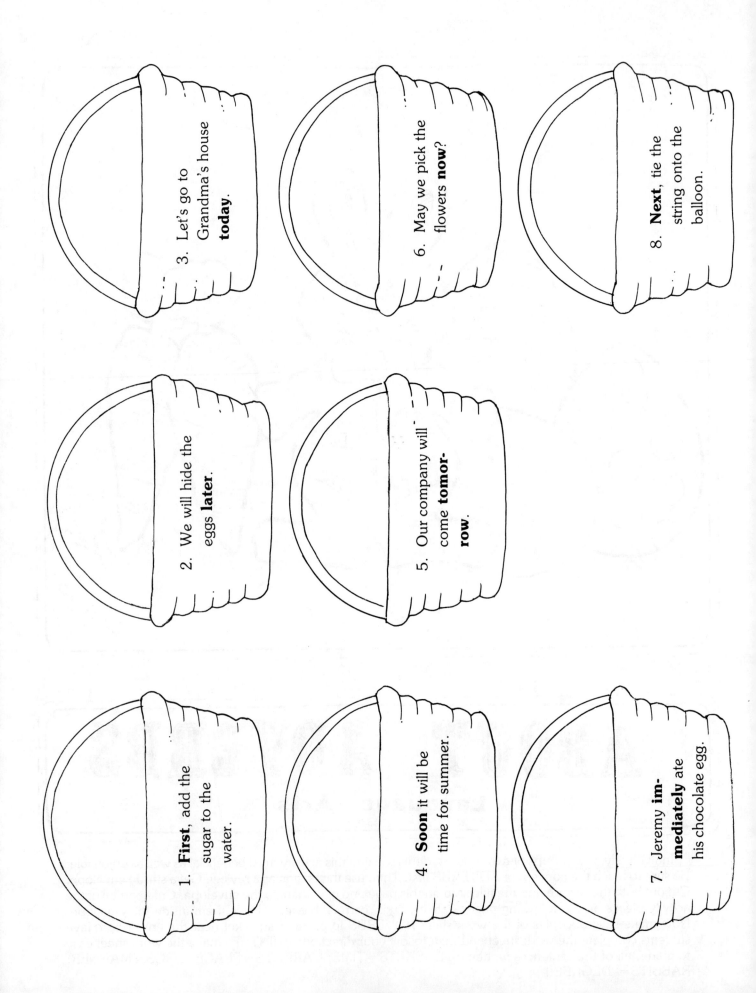

3. Let's go to Grandma's house **today**.

6. May we pick the flowers **now**?

8. **Next**, tie the string onto the balloon.

2. We will hide the eggs **later**.

5. Our company will come **tomorrow**.

1. **First**, add the sugar to the water.

4. **Soon** it will be time for summer.

7. Jeremy **immediately** ate his chocolate egg.

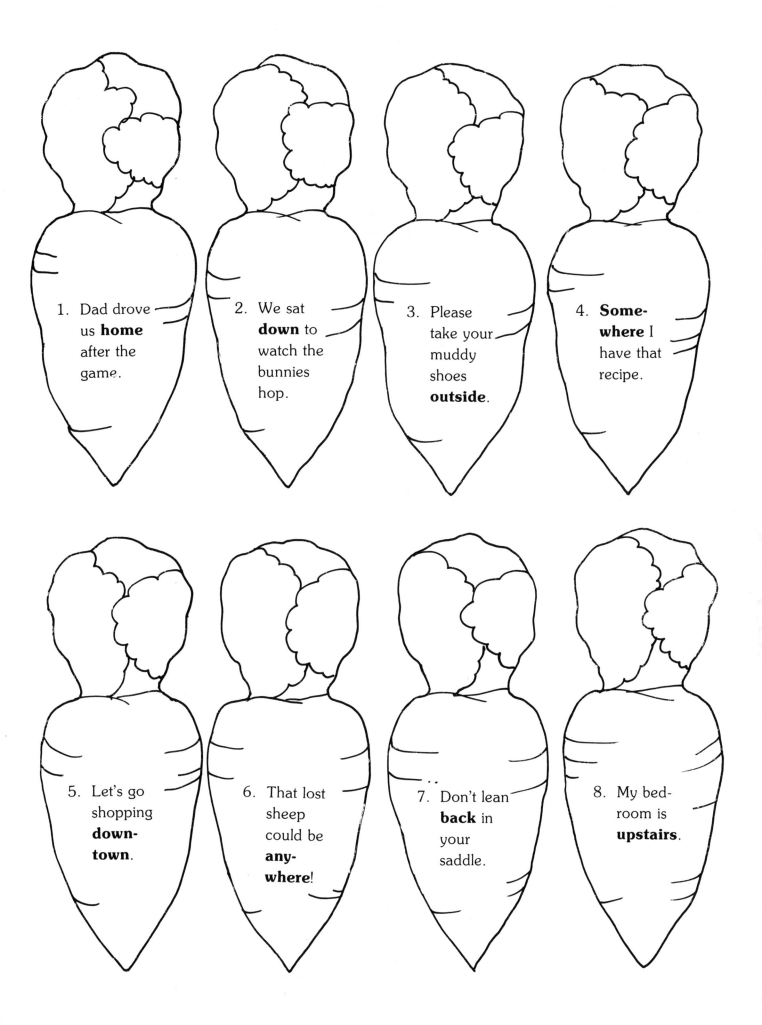

1. Dad drove us **home** after the game.

2. We sat **down** to watch the bunnies hop.

3. Please take your muddy shoes **outside**.

4. **Somewhere** I have that recipe.

5. Let's go shopping **downtown**.

6. That lost sheep could be **anywhere**!

7. Don't lean **back** in your saddle.

8. My bedroom is **upstairs**.

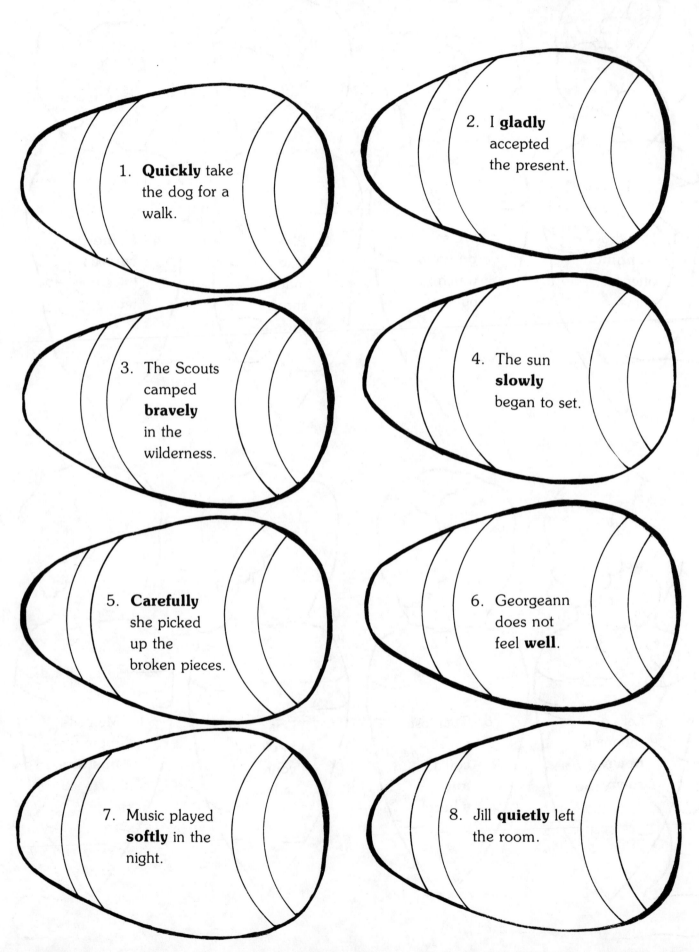

1. **Quickly** take the dog for a walk.

2. I **gladly** accepted the present.

3. The Scouts camped **bravely** in the wilderness.

4. The sun **slowly** began to set.

5. **Carefully** she picked up the broken pieces.

6. Georgeann does not feel **well**.

7. Music played **softly** in the night.

8. Jill **quietly** left the room.

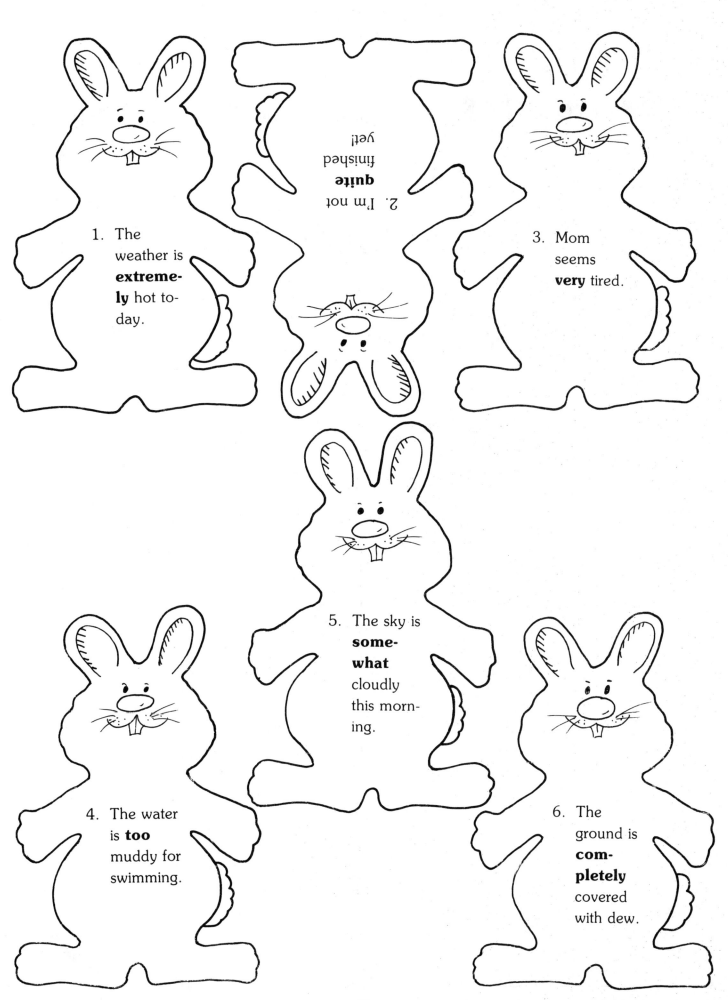

1. The weather is **extreme-ly** hot to-day.

2. I'm not **quite** finished yet!

3. Mom seems **very** tired.

5. The sky is **some-what** cloudly this morn-ing.

4. The water is **too** muddy for swimming.

6. The ground is **com-pletely** covered with dew.

57

Adverbs

answer the questions HOW, WHEN, WHERE, and HOW MUCH or TO WHAT DEGREE.

Read these examples:

1. **Tomorrow** Mom is going to bake bread. (**Tomorrow** is an adverb telling WHEN)
2. That bird **swiftly** flew past the window. (**Swiftly** is an adverb telling HOW.)
3. Please come **downstairs** and answer the door. (**Downstairs** is an adverb telling WHERE.)
4. I am **totally** confused. (**Totally** is an adverb telling TO WHAT DEGREE.)

Take all of the activity pieces out of the envelope. Read each sentence and decide which question the bold adverb answers. Write the adverb in the correct space on the chart below.

ADVERBS

Time	Place	Manner	Degree

STRICTLY BUSINESS

1 Rabbit Road
O'Hare, Illinois 62417
April 1, 1987

Mr. Ronald Duck
345 Swallow Lake
Whitewater, West Virginia 26521

Dear Mr. Duck:

   In the library last week I found a copy of your latest book *This Quacks Me Up*. I enjoyed reading the jokes in it and would like to buy a copy of it for my own collection here at home. Please send me a copy of the book to the address above. Enclosed you will find $7.50. Could you also send me the latest catalog of all of your books? Thank you.

Sincerely yours,

Hugs Bunny

.. .. ..JUST WRITE.. .. .. ..

Addresses which follow are from *Free Stuff for Kids*, Meadowbrook Press, Deephaven, MN 55391, 1981 and *Freebies for Kids* by Jeffrey Feinman, Wanderer Books, published by Simon & Schuster, Inc., NY, 1983.

Brief history of Jolly Time popcorn and 20 popcorn recipes. Send 25¢ with your name and address to:

    Jolly Time Popcorn Recipes
    Box 178
    Sioux City, IA 51102

Play clay can easily be molded to create terrific crafts for yourself or friends. Write to:

    Play Clay Play
    Dept. PC-N, Box 307
    Coventry, CT 06238

How to create a flower arrangement (guide). Send for Circular #1020 (Flower Arranging) and enclose 15¢ to:

    University of Illinois Agricultural
      Publication
    College of Agriculture
    1301 Gregory Drive
    Urbana, IL 61801

Enjoy seasonal fun by doing, using this fun booklet of activities. Write for a copy of "Doing Is Fun." Enclose a #10-sized envelope (self-addressed) to:

    The Garden Club of America
    598 Madison Avenue
    New York, NY 10022

Recycle old containers to make some Crafty Critters. Send for "Crafty Critters" on a postcard to:

    Texize
    P.O. Box 368
    Greenville, SC 29602

Bird-watching poster that will bring wildlife to your classroom. Send a legal-sized self-addressed stamped envelope to:

    The Garden Club of America
    598 Madison Avenue
    New York, NY 10022

A pamphlet giving instructions on how to create a train full of animals. Send for "Zoo Train Animals," free of charge to:

    Animal Cutouts
    c/o Georgia-Pacific
    P. O. Box 12091
    Portland, OR 97212

Two booklets—"Birdwatching" and "Recycle for the Birds"—can be yours for $1.00 and a request for Publication #79258 to:

    National Wildlife Federation
    Dept. 152
    1412 16th Street, NW
    Washington, D.C. 20036

"Craft Ideas" is a booklet of ideas made from household materials. Send a postcard to:

    Johnson Wax
    Consumer Education
    P.O. Box 567, Dept. RC-FK
    Racine, WI 53401

Learn about birds. Send a legal-sized self-addressed stamped envelope for "Berried Treasure for Your Birds" to:

    The Garden Club of America
    598 Madison Avenue
    New York, NY 10022

"You and Your Dog" pamphlet. Write to:

Animal Welfare Institute
P. O. Box 3650
Washington, D.C. 20007

"Kittens and Cat" pamphlet. Write to:

Animal Welfare Institute
P.O. Box 3650
Washington, D.C. 20007

Learn about horses in this booklet. Write for "Youth Activities" to:

American Quarter Horse Association
Amarillo, TX 79168

The story of the Bronx Zoo and the animals that live there. Send to:

The Bronx Zoo
New York Zoological Society
185th Street & Southern Blvd.
Bronx, NY 10460

A fifty-four page, colorful booklet loaded with activities for garden fun. Send 50¢ to:

Chevron Chemical Company
575 Market Street
San Francisco, CA 94105

Learn about light and color with these rainbow glasses. Send 75¢ to:

Mr. Rainbow
P.O. Box 27056
Philadelphia, PA 19118

Learn about clouds with this full color cloud chart. Send $1.00 and a self-addressed stamped envelope to:

C.C. Marketing
P.O. Box 1122
Glen Allen, VA 23060

Order this kaleidaglas kit to see a world full of rainbows. Ask for Kaleidaglas Glasses Kit and send 50¢ to:

The Holex Corporation
Dept. RB
P.O. Box 27056
Philadelphia, PA 19118

Use a postcard to receive a booklet about how to invite birds to your home. Ask for *Invite Birds to Your Home: Conservation Plantings for the* . . .

1. Northwest
2. Northeast
3. Midwest
4. Southeast
(State your area. None available for Southwest.)

Write to:

Soil Conservation Service
Room 0054
P.O. Box 2890
Washington, D.C. 20013

PICTURE THIS

TO CREATE THE BULLETIN BOARD, YOU WILL NEED:

1. Scissors
2. Pencils
3. Crayons or markers
4. Glue
5. Large sheet of construction paper (12″ × 18″)
6. A copy of the work sheet "Picture This"

Read each step carefully before going on to the next step.

1. Color each object on page 64.
2. Carefully cut each object out along the dotted lines.
3. Get a large piece of light-colored construction paper (12″ × 18″) and turn it sideways in front of you. With your pencil, label the top of your paper N (North), the right side of your paper E (East), the bottom of your paper S (South), and the left side of your paper W (West).
4. In the very center of your paper, glue the TREE.
5. To the right of the tree draw a POND.
6. Add a swimming DUCK to your pond.
7. In the SW corner of your paper draw a TREE like the one glued on your paper.
8. To the right of the tree paste the RABBIT with his back toward you.
9. In the center at the bottom of your paper draw a side view of a CART with only two wheels. (Only one wheel will show.) Draw the cart's handles on the right side.
10. Glue the CARROT to the other rabbit's hand.
11. Paste the RABBIT holding the carrot near the handles of the cart.
12. Inside the cart place the two large EGGS.
13. Draw GRASS in the cart around the eggs and all across the bottom of your paper.
14. To the left of the center tree, and a little south, glue the BASKET with eggs.
15. To the right of the duck pond, paste the LAMB.
16. Draw GRASS around the center tree, the lamb, and the duck pond.
17. Add five FLOWERS to the SE section of your paper. Draw GRASS near them.
18. Color any object that is not yet colored on your paper.
19. Write your name on the back of your paper.
20. Give your completed project to your teacher.

Mixed-Up Stories

Cut apart all of the sentence strips, one paragraph at a time. On a separate sheet of paper, glue the sentences in the correct order. When you finish, you should have three complete paragraphs. Then choose one paragraph to copy in correct paragraph form.

1.
| We packed our lunch and set out. |
| It was there we discovered the bags of stolen money. |
| After walking for a few hours through the dense woods, we came to a beautiful lake. |
| Boy, would the police be happy to hear our story! |
| One spring morning my best friend and I decided to go hiking. |

2.
| Just as we reached the park, it began to rain again. |
| I put on my baseball uniform and gulped down supper. |
| The rain stopped and it looked as though our game would be played as scheduled. |
| When I closed the screen door, there stood Ron. |
| I grabbed my hat and glove. |

3.
| Everyone else had gone to bed. |
| I got my snacks and sat down on the sofa, munching on popcorn. |
| My popcorn flew everywhere. |
| I was too scared to move. |
| Last night I decided to stay up late and watch TV. |
| I wanted to see a scary movie. |
| Suddenly, someone screamed. |

Draw each step shown above to create your own little rabbit. Color it.

FACTS

Here are basic facts for you to use in your story. Use the space below to add more details in each category, to help organize your thoughts and to make your writing more interesting.

Who   RABBITS

What PARTY

When MORNING

Where RABBIT HOLLOW

Why   TO CELEBRATE

A TALE TO TELL

MULTIPLE CHOICE

Circle the letter of the answer which correctly completes the pattern begun.

1. 3, 6, 9, 12,
    A. 14, 16, 18
    B. 15, 18, 21
    C. 13, 16, 19

2. 7, 14, 21, 28,
    A. 32, 39, 45
    B. 35, 42, 49
    C. 34, 41, 47

3. 2, 4, 6, 8,
    A. 10, 12, 14
    B. 9, 10, 11
    C. 12, 14, 16

4. 10, 20, 30, 40
    A. 41, 42, 43
    B. 45, 50, 55
    C. 50, 60, 70

5. 4, 8, 12, 16
    A. 18, 22, 26
    B. 17, 18, 19
    C. 20, 24, 28

6. 11, 22, 33, 44,
    A. 55, 66, 77
    B. 45, 46, 47
    C. 53, 64, 75

7. 5, 10, 15, 20,
    A. 30, 40, 50
    B. 25, 30, 35
    C. 21, 22, 23

8. 9, 18, 27, 36,
    A. 37, 38, 39
    B. 42, 49, 56
    C. 45, 54, 63

9. 6, 12, 18, 24,
    A. 32, 38, 44
    B. 30, 36, 42
    C. 29, 35, 41

10. 8, 16, 24, 32,
    A. 34, 36, 38
    B. 39, 46, 54
    C. 40, 48, 56

11. 12, 24, 36, 48,
    A. 60, 72, 84
    B. 52, 58, 64
    C. 62, 74, 92

Boy Puppet

Girl Puppet

COPYCAT

WHAT FUN

Dad said I could go outside
And leave my jacket opened wide.

And Mom said I could stay all day
And not do any work—just play.

My sister said she'd feed the dog
And clean the cage of my pet frog.

My brother said he'd do my chores
And let me use his fishing lures.

My grandpa gave me his rod and reel;
You don't know how good that made me feel!

My teacher said there would be no school—
APRIL FOOL!

A STRING BASKET

TO MAKE THIS DELIGHTFUL, DECORATIVE BASKET, YOU WILL NEED:

1. large coffee can
2. white glue
3. water
4. colored crochet thread
5. small jar lid
6. lace trim
7. scissors
8. Easter grass
9. balloon (one per child)
10. candy
11. old newspapers
12. spoon

DIRECTIONS:

1. Place newspapers around your work area.

2. Get a large coffee can. Fill it about ⅓ full of warm water. Add white glue and stir until water looks milky and glue is well mixed.

3. Now cut a piece of crochet thread (or thin string) to a length of about six feet. Put the cut string into the can and gently stir so that all thread is well-coated.

4. Blow up a balloon. Tie it.

5. Now find the end of your thread and carefully wrap it around your balloon, turning your balloon constantly as you cover it. Don't cover it completely, but be sure that there are no large uncovered spots.

6. Your balloon must now dry for a few days. Hang it somewhere in the room from the knot so that the thread can dry freely.

7. Once your balloon has dried, pop the balloon if it hasn't already popped.

8. Carefully cut a hole along the side of your balloon so that you can put Easter grass and candy in it.

9. Next take your jar lid and glue the outer rim. Attach lace or other trim to this rim. The lid will serve as a base to keep your balloon from rolling around.

10. You may also want to add lace trim to the edge of the hole you cut on your basket, but this is optional.

11. Arrange grass in the basket, add candy, decorations, or whatever you like.

12. Display your completed basket on the lid and enjoy it.

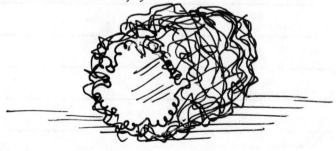

B O O K

R E P O R T

by: _____

Plot:
_____
_____
_____
_____
_____
_____
_____
_____
_____
_____
_____

Best Part:
_____
_____
_____
_____
_____
_____
_____
_____
_____

Title:
_____

Author: _____

Setting: _____
_____

Characters: _____
_____
_____
_____
_____

A Hare Racing Event

start

end

PLAYERS: 2-5

DIRECTIONS: Place all game cards on the game-board, face down. Player 1 flips a penny. Heads—move ahead one space; tails—move ahead two spaces. Another player asks the question. If student answers correctly, he moves the correct number of spaces. If incorrect, he moves back that number of spaces. Used game cards are placed on bottom of pile. First player around the board wins.

Game cards

ALABAMA	ALASKA	ARIZONA
ARKANSAS	CALIFORNIA	COLORADO
CONNECTICUT	DELAWARE	FLORIDA
GEORGIA	HAWAII	IDAHO
ILLINOIS	INDIANA	IOWA
KANSAS	KENTUCKY	LOUISIANA
MAINE	MARYLAND	MASSACHUSETTS
MICHIGAN	MINNESOTA	MISSISSIPPI

MISSOURI	MONTANA	NEBRASKA
NEVADA	NEW HAMPSHIRE	NEW JERSEY
NEW MEXICO	NEW YORK	NORTH CAROLINA
NORTH DAKOTA	OHIO	OKLAHOMA
OREGON	PENNSYLVANIA	RHODE ISLAND
SOUTH CAROLINA	SOUTH DAKOTA	TENNESSEE
TEXAS	UTAH	VERMONT
VIRGINIA	WASHINGTON	WEST VIRGINIA

WISCONSIN	WYOMING	Mount Rushmore
Grand Canyon	Golden Gate Bridge	Orange Bowl
Disneyland	Mt. McKinley	Myrtle Beach
Glacier National Park	Alamo	Gateway to the West (Arch)
Empire State Building	Superdome	Cape Cod
Space Needle	Sears Tower	Rose Bowl
Liberty Bell	Green Mountains	Wall Street

Game Pieces

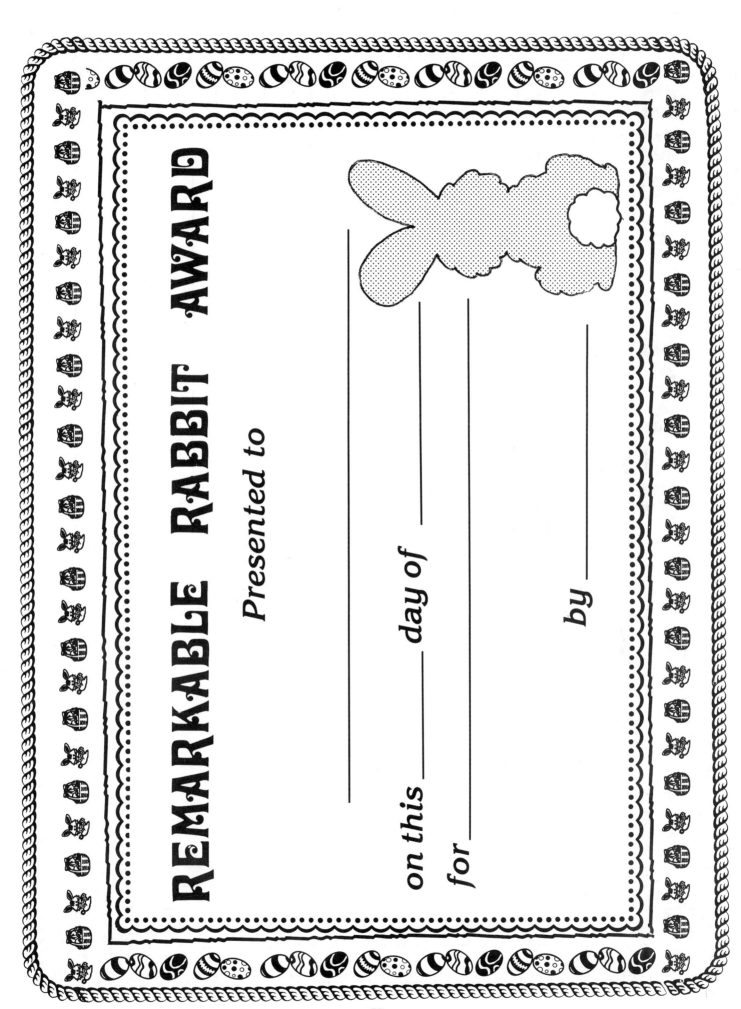

REMARKABLE RABBIT AWARD

Presented to

_____

on this _____ day of _____

for _____

by _____

REPORT CARD

FOR _____

ACTIVITY	COMMENT
1. Dress the Rabbit	
2. Quack-Ups	
3. Scrambled Eggs	
4. About Adverbs	
5. Strictly Business	
6. Picture This	
7. Mixed-Up Stories	
8. Facts/A Tale to Tell	
9. Multiple Choice	
10. Puppet	
11. Copycat	
12. A String Basket	
13. Book Report	
14. A Hare Racing Event	
15.	
16.	
17.	
18.	

Here are the activities included in this unit. Circle each lesson that you complete and be sure to put all work in its proper place so that your teacher can check it. Follow all directions for each activity. If you do any additional activities, be sure to add them to the list below after you make proper arrangements with your teacher.

1. Dress the Rabbit
2. Quack-Ups
3. Scrambled Eggs
4. About Adverbs
5. Strictly Business
6. Picture This
7. Mixed-Up Stories
8. Facts/A Tale to Tell
9. Multiple Choice
10. Puppets
11. Copycat
12. A String Basket
13. Book Report
14. A Hare Racing Event
15.
16.
17.
18.

Your Grade:

A = 15 or more activities well-done
B = 11-14
C = 8-10
D = 5-7
E = less than 4

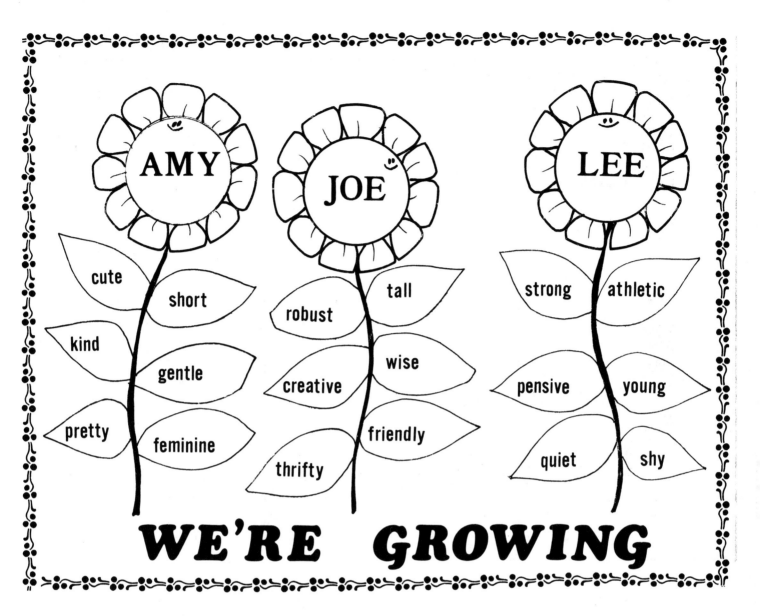

WE'RE GROWING

TO CREATE THE BULLETIN BOARD, YOU WILL NEED:

1. A large sheet of yellow or pale-blue background paper.
2. Patterns for the letters in the title which can be found on the following pages.
3. Large pieces of construction paper in bright colors for the flowers.
4. Green construction paper for the stems and leaves.

PRACTICAL USES:

1. Give each student a flower, stem, and several leaves. Have children draw names. Each will write the name of the student he selected in the center of the flower. After he glues on the stem, have him attach leaves. Tell children to write adjectives on the various leaves to describe the persons they chose. Display completed flowers on the bulletin board.
2. Write a number from 1-12 on the center of each flower. Place a packet of leaves on the bulletin board. Have children place the correct leaves on the flower to show multiples of the number displayed. Leave an answer key in the packet.
3. Place a number in the center of each flower. Have students place the correct addends or factors (leaves) on the correct stems. (Again place answer key nearby).
4. Use the bulletin board as a language arts station. Write a word in the center of each flower, and let children add synonyms or antonyms to the leaves.

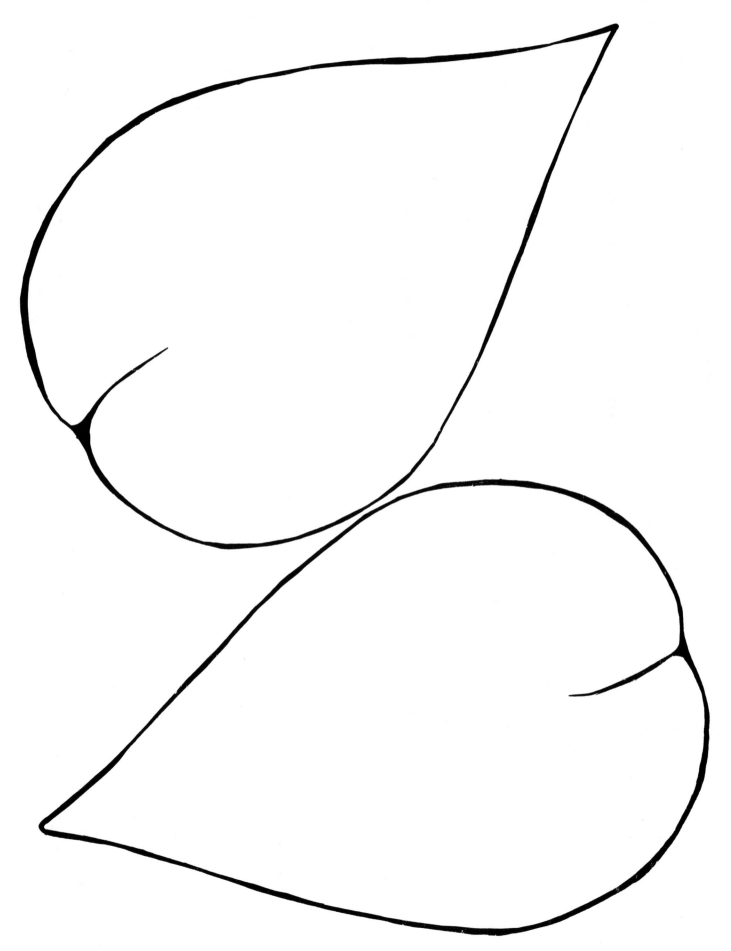

DOOR KNOCKER

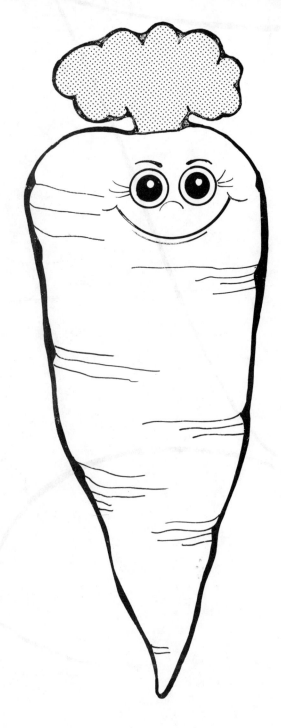

Your classroom door will be quite an attraction this spring. Title it "What's Up, Doc?"

Place a large, colored carrot which you have laminated on your door. Give each student a carrot pattern found on the following page. Ask each child to write a riddle on the outside of his carrot, and write the answer to the riddle inside. Have the student write his name on the carrot top.

Now ask each child to fold his carrot in half on the fold lines. Have him glue Tab A to Tab B and press firmly until the glue sticks. In this way, the answer to the riddle can be easily read while the completed projects are displayed on the classroom door.

You may wish to have students write more than one riddle, so that carrots can be changed often.

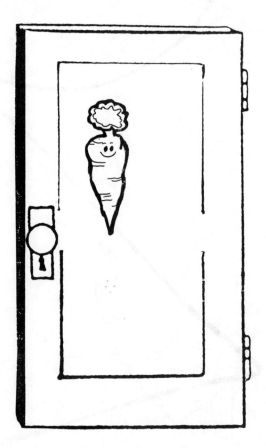

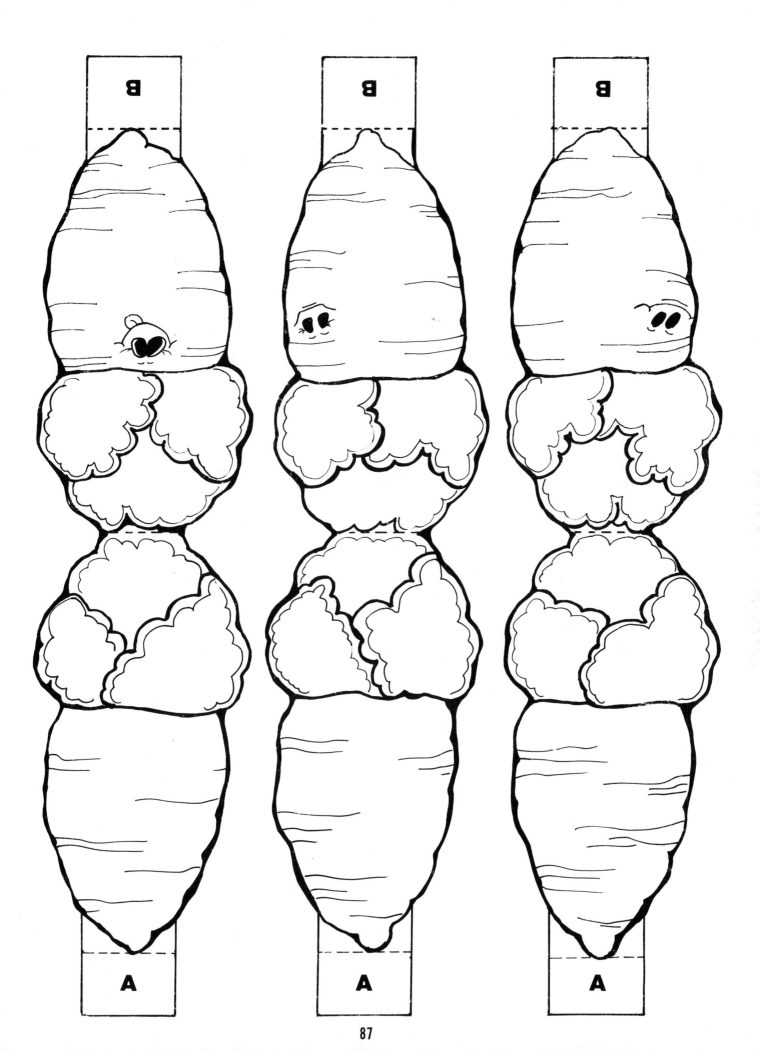

ANTicipation

TO CREATE THE BULLETIN BOARD, YOU WILL NEED:

1. A large sheet of light-blue background paper.
2. Patterns for the letters in the title which can be found on the following pages.
3. Green grass made from a sheet of large paper. Crepe paper cut and fringed could be used to add texture.
4. Pieces of black construction paper can be used for making the large ants. Pipe cleaners can be used for the legs and antenna. "Googoo eyes," available at craft and fabric stores, could be glued to the construction paper heads to add a touch of whimsy.
5. The picnic foods could be made from construction paper, or actual pictures of foods could be cut from magazine advertisements.

PRACTICAL USES:

1. Have a class discussion on the word *anticipation*. What are the feelings involved when one is anticipating a trip to the dentist, an approaching birthday, the coming of summer, a first dive into a lake, or receiving a report card. Have students write about one of their most vivid anticipations.
2. Attach a folder to each food displayed on the bulletin board. Activity sheets could focus on Dictionary Work (beginning, middle, end); Parts of Speech (noun, verb, adjective); Math Problems (simple, average, difficult); Creative Writing (topic, development, closure).

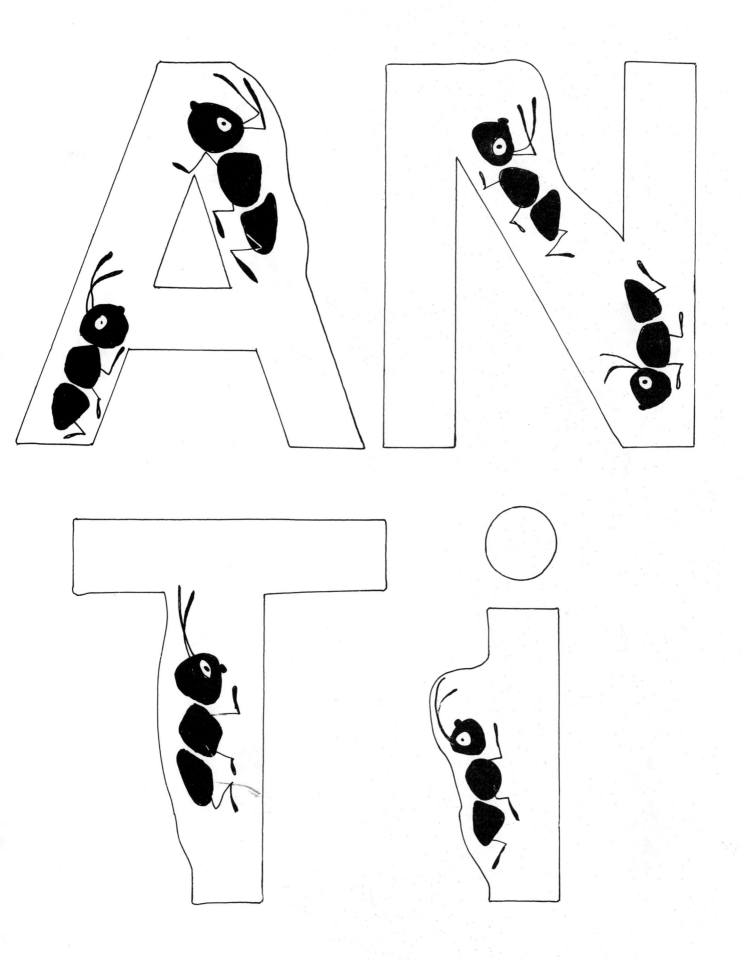

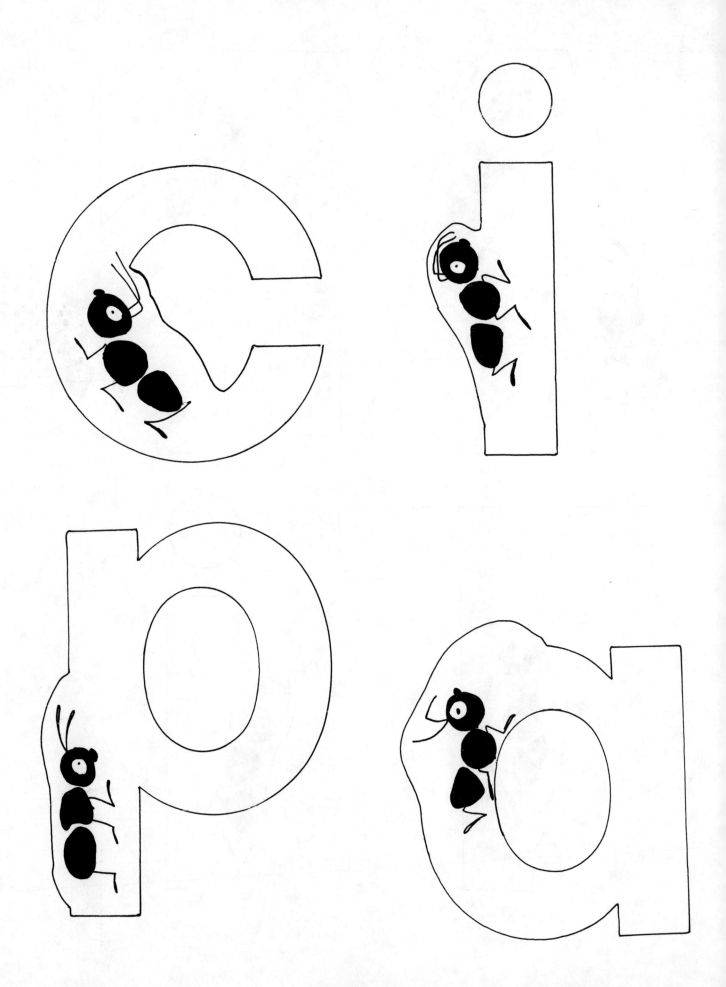

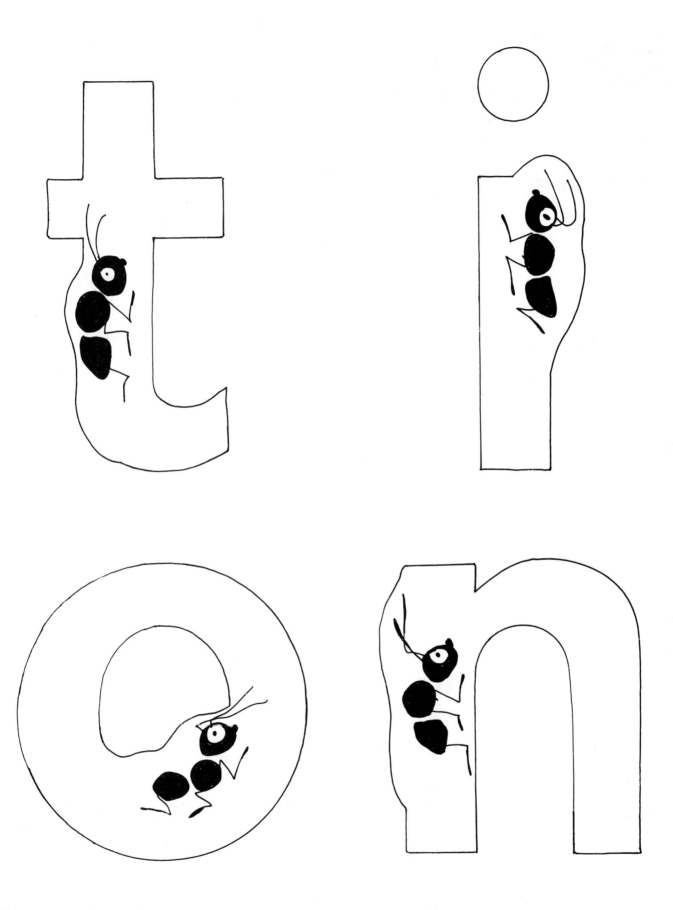

SPELLING IS A

Write a symbol after each letter of the alphabet to create a code. Then choose any fourteen of your spelling words for the week to write in code. Give your paper to a friend to solve.

A *   B ■   C ø   D   E   F   G   H

I   J   K   L   M   N   O   P

Q   R   S   T   U   V   W   X

Y   Z   1_____   2_____

_____   _____

3 _____   4 _____   5 _____

_____   _____   _____

6 _____   7 _____   8 _____

_____   _____   _____

9 _____   10 _____   11 _____

_____   _____   _____

12 _____   13 _____   14 _____

_____   _____   _____

PIECE OF CAKE

"ANT"ONYMS

Read each sentence below. In the blank write the opposite of the word you see in parentheses.

1. The bus left (early) _____ for the school picnic.

2. It was the (last) _____ time we had gone to Holly Park.

3. The children were (sad) _____ about going.

4. (Few) _____ boys and girls were singing songs.

5. This was going to be a (short) _____ bus ride.

6. Most of the seats on the bus were (empty) _____.

7. (None) _____ of the children were glad it was Saturday.

8. When the bus stopped, it was time to get (on) _____.

9. The children (walked) _____ to the picnic tables to eat.

10. They ate their lunches (slowly) _____.

11. Ants crawled on the table where the (grown-ups) _____ ate.

12. (Girls) _____ began to throw Frisbees.

13. One girl tried to (throw) _____ it.

14. (Before) _____ they ate, it was time for a visit to the zoo.

15. Most of the animals were (inside) _____.

16. The monkeys were the (quietest) _____ of all the animals.

17. Later the kids (sold) _____ souvenirs.

18. Several boys got on the (right) _____ bus.

19. It was (morning) _____ when the children got back to school.

20. The sky was beginning to get (light) _____.

Circle the word in each row that is **opposite** the first word.

1. messy   sloppy, neat, dirty
2. soft   mushy, weak, hard
3. pretty   ugly, beautiful, lovely
4. old   worn, used, new
5. smooth   level, rough, flat

"ANT"icipating a Work of Art

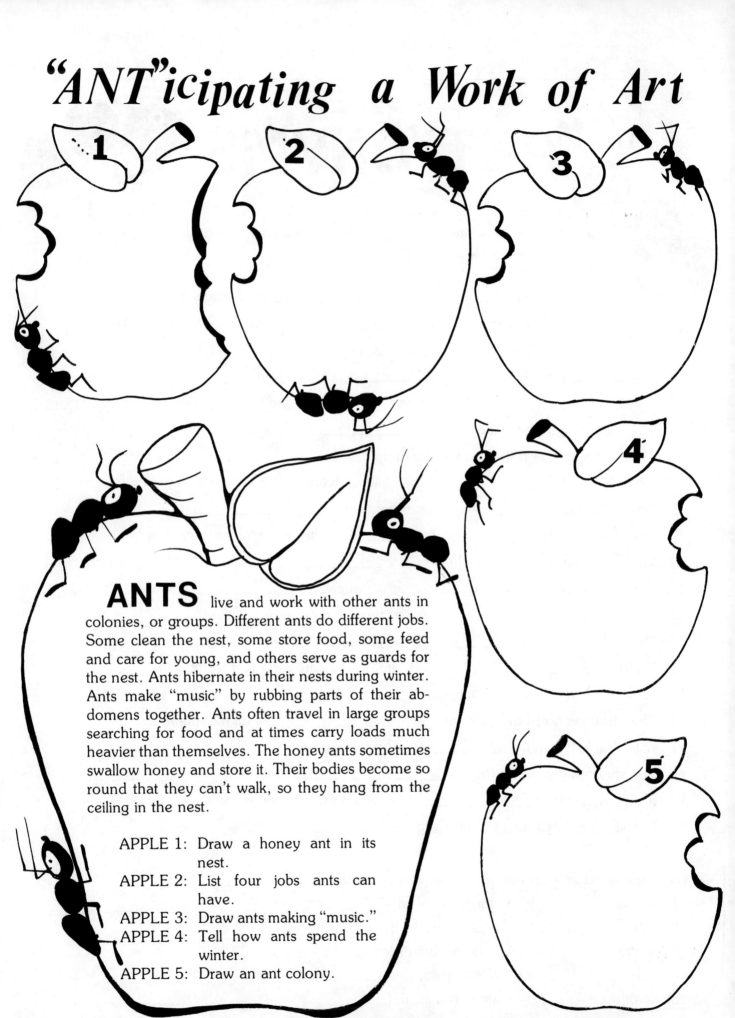

ANTS live and work with other ants in colonies, or groups. Different ants do different jobs. Some clean the nest, some store food, some feed and care for young, and others serve as guards for the nest. Ants hibernate in their nests during winter. Ants make "music" by rubbing parts of their abdomens together. Ants often travel in large groups searching for food and at times carry loads much heavier than themselves. The honey ants sometimes swallow honey and store it. Their bodies become so round that they can't walk, so they hang from the ceiling in the nest.

APPLE 1: Draw a honey ant in its nest.
APPLE 2: List four jobs ants can have.
APPLE 3: Draw ants making "music."
APPLE 4: Tell how ants spend the winter.
APPLE 5: Draw an ant colony.

WE'RE BACK !

Directions: Write the bold word in the correct jar.

One pretty day in the month of **May**
My **friends** and **I** went **out** to play.
We **walked** so **slowly** to **the** park;
There children laugh and puppies bark.
Hot dogs were roasting on the grill,
We **smelled them** as we climbed the hill.
The table sitting by the stream
Was sure to be any picnicker's dream.
We **found** some cakes, salads, chips, pies,
They looked so glorious to our **hungry eyes**.
I **discovered** the chef asleep on a stool,
The grown-ups and **kids** took a swim in the pool.
We climbed on the table and just ate a bite,
But one led to another, then oh! What a sight!
We **ate** such a **feast**, crumbs fell to the ground.
Not one of **us noticed** the **approaching** sound
Of the chef coming **swiftly**, his feet doing **a** dance,
The look on his face when **he** saw us—BLACK **ANTS**!
We looked like **an** army, so **quickly** retreating,
Our bellies were full after all of that eating.
We **marched** to our colony, **burrowed inside**,
Until the **next picnic**—we'll stay **here** and hide.

NOUNS

1. _____
2. _____
3. _____
4. _____
5. _____
6. _____
7. _____
8. _____

VERBS

1. _____
2. _____
3. _____
4. _____
5. _____
6. _____
7. _____
8. _____

ADVERBS

1. _____
2. _____
3. _____
4. _____
5. _____
6. _____
7. _____
8. _____

ADJECTIVES

1. _____
2. _____
3. _____
4. _____
5. _____
6. _____
7. _____
8. _____

PRONOUNS

1. _____
2. _____
3. _____
4. _____
5. _____
6. _____

ANT FUN

All of us have seen ants—on the ground, in trees, and sometimes in our houses. But have you noticed how different one ant can be from another? The best way to observe ants is to put them into a nest where they will form a COLONY.

Locate an anthill and get many ants. Put the sand, soil and ants into a jar. (Don't mix ants from different colonies, because they will fight.) Place the jar in a pan of water so the ants will not escape beyond the water. Tie paper around the jar. In a few days the ants will tunnel close to the sides. Keep this ant home at room temperature away from the direct sunlight.

Feed the ants bits of apple, caterpillars, and freshly killed insects. Give them water on a small sponge.

Bite into Addition

1
```
 80,167
+78,945
```

2
```
  317
  884
+209
```

3
```
 4651
+3786
```

4
```
  591
  769
+128
```

5
```
  674
  309
+716
```

6
```
 1357
 8642
+9065
```

7
```
 9126
+7854
```

8
```
  215
  658
+907
```

Plot:

Book Report

by: _____

Best Part:

Title: _____
Author: _____
Setting: _____
Characters: _____

FOOTLOOSE

TO CREATE THE BULLETIN BOARD, YOU WILL NEED:

1. A large sheet of light-blue background paper.
2. Patterns for the letters in the title which can be found on the following pages.
3. Light-colored construction paper for the worm head with antennae (pattern follows).
4. Light-colored construction paper for the body segments with feet (one copy per child).
5. Paper fasteners to attach construction paper or oaktag feet to the segments.

PRACTICAL USES:

1. The title of the bulletin board suggests a variety of uses. Use the bulletin board to display goals of students as they are promoted to a higher grade or as they move to another school via graduation.

    Write the alphabet or numbers on the segments to show sequencing.

    In September have children write short biographical sketches to display on their segments so others may learn more about them.

2. Move the worm to a large wall in the room where it can "grow." Use it for book reports, vocabulary words, letters, or other activities which are cumulative.

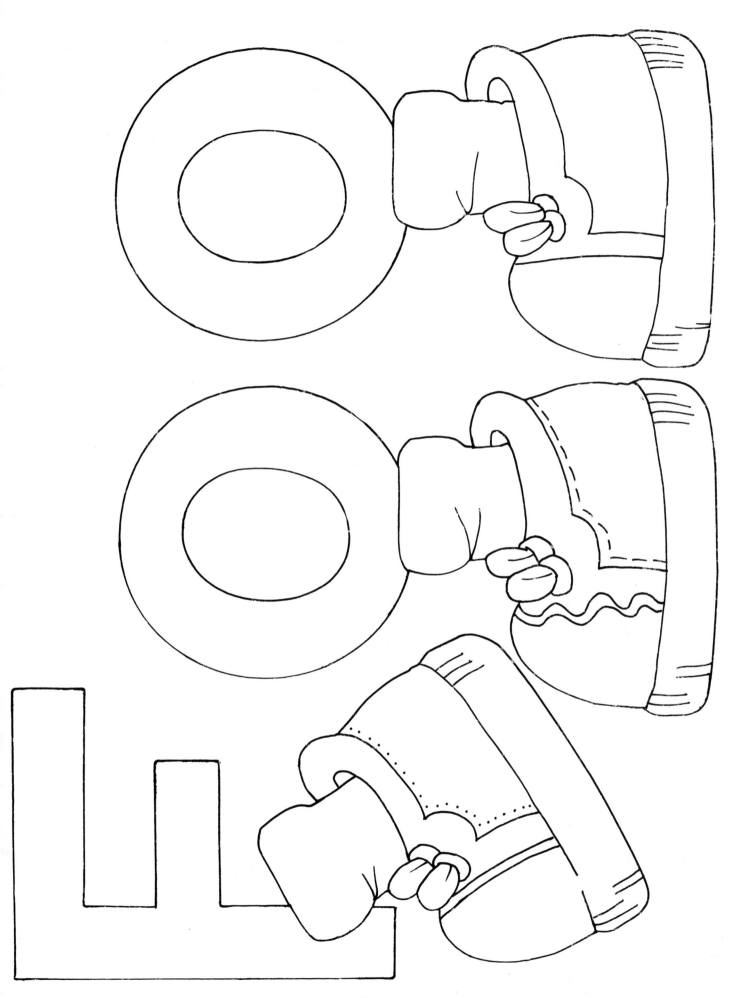

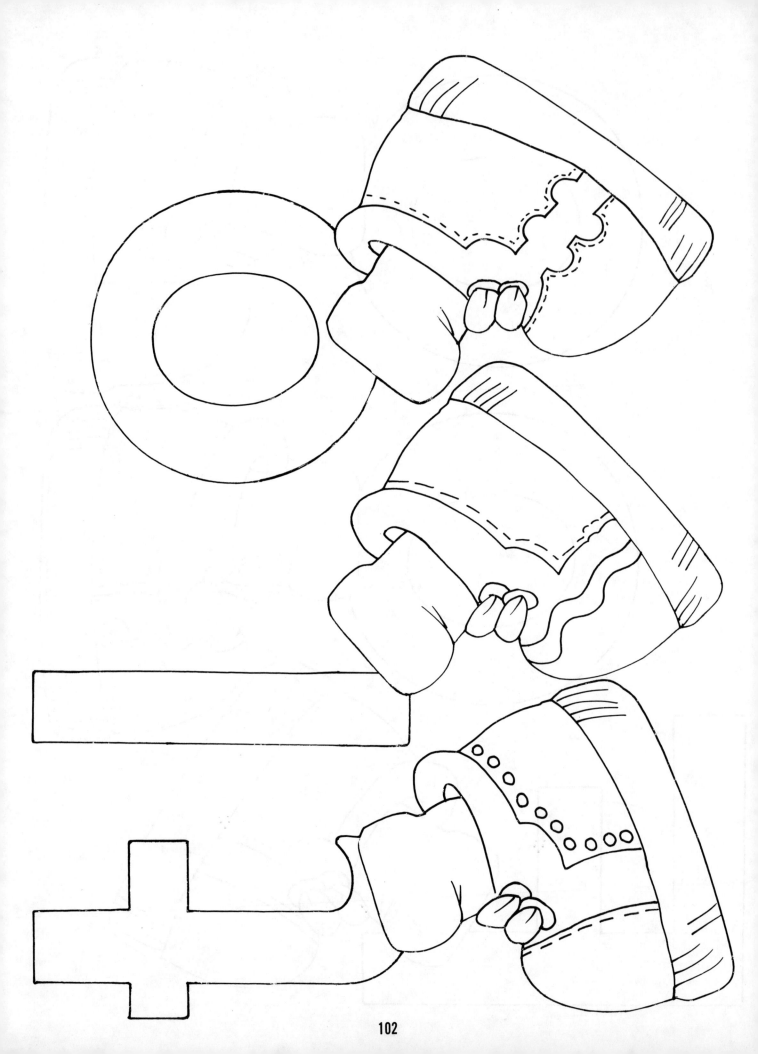

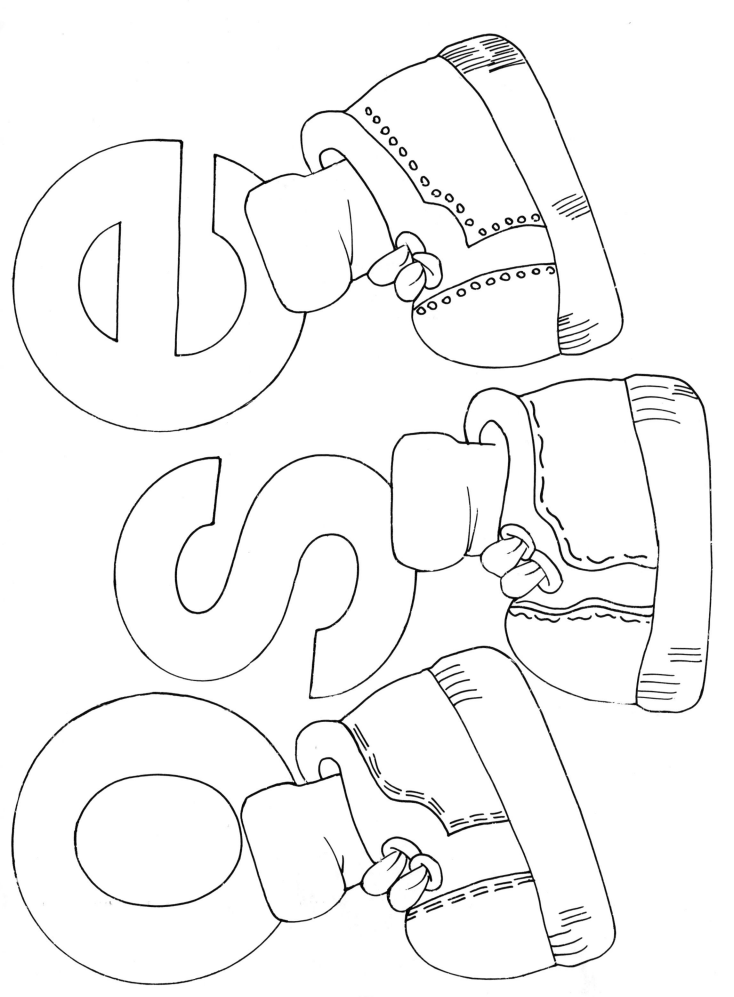

HEAD

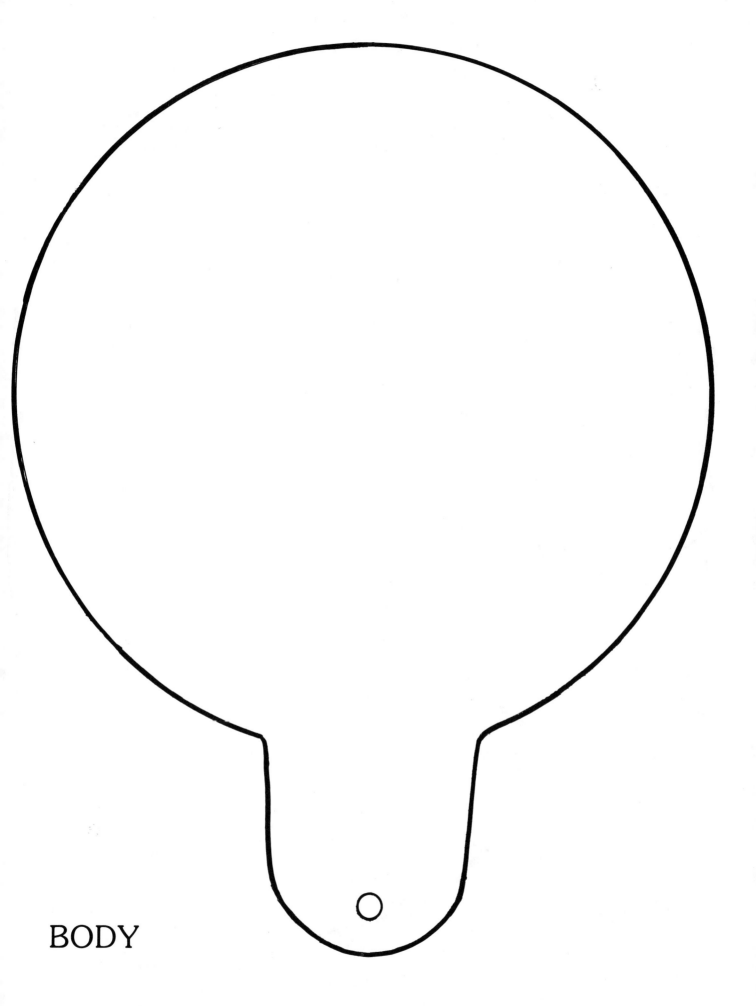

BODY

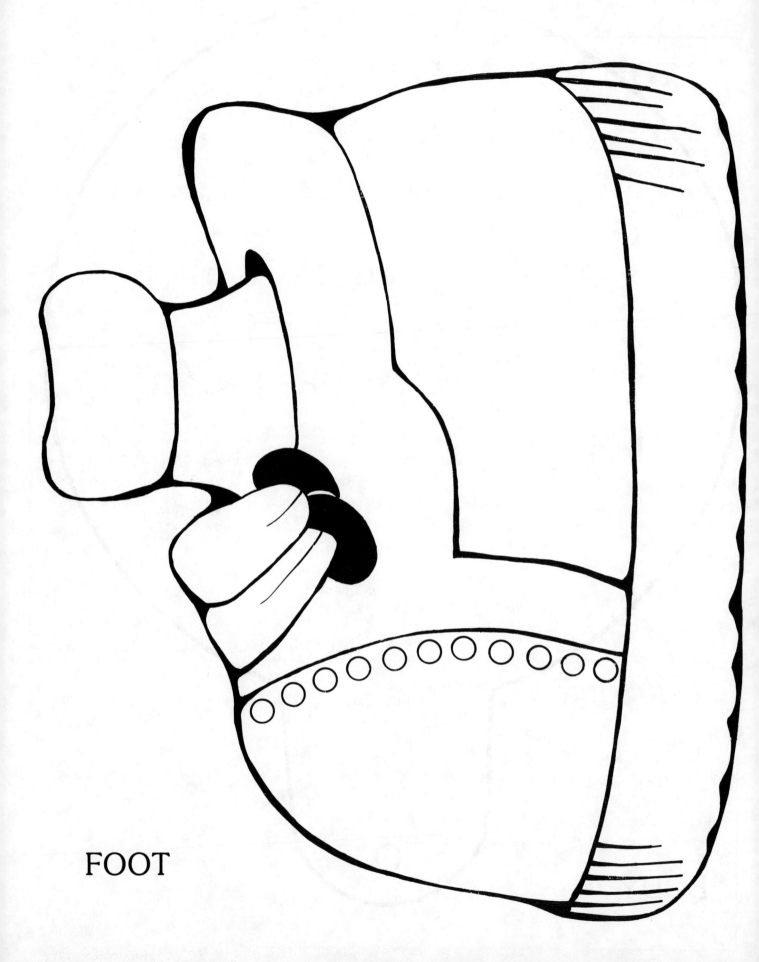

FOOT

"TOE"L PAINTING

What a terrific way to get students involved. Give each child a large piece of art paper, put several containers of paint on the floor beside paper. Have student sit on a chair and "paint" a scene or object with his toe. Put an old rag and a container of water by the chair.

SHOE DESIGNING

With designer fashions in vogue, this art project will surely capture your students' attention. Give each child art paper and crayons. Have him design a shoe of his choice or several shoes for various occasions. Let him color the shoe after he designs it. Fabric can also be used.

FOOTPRINTING

Children love graffiti and the outdoors, so combine these favorites for an art activity. Have students work in groups using large sheets of butcher or shelf paper. Place several large containers of poster paint, water, and old rags nearby. Tell students to "print" messages to others with their feet.

THE FOOTLOCKER

Dramatics

Here is an activity your whole class can enjoy. Feel free to add ideas of your own or those of your students when doing creative dramatics. Get a sturdy envelope. Cut out both the picture and the title strip on this page and glue them to the envelope. Cut apart the feet on the following pages. Place them inside the envelope. Ask children, one at a time, to come to the front of the group, select a foot, study it, and then act out the message given for other students to guess. Additional ideas can be written on the reverse sides of the feet.

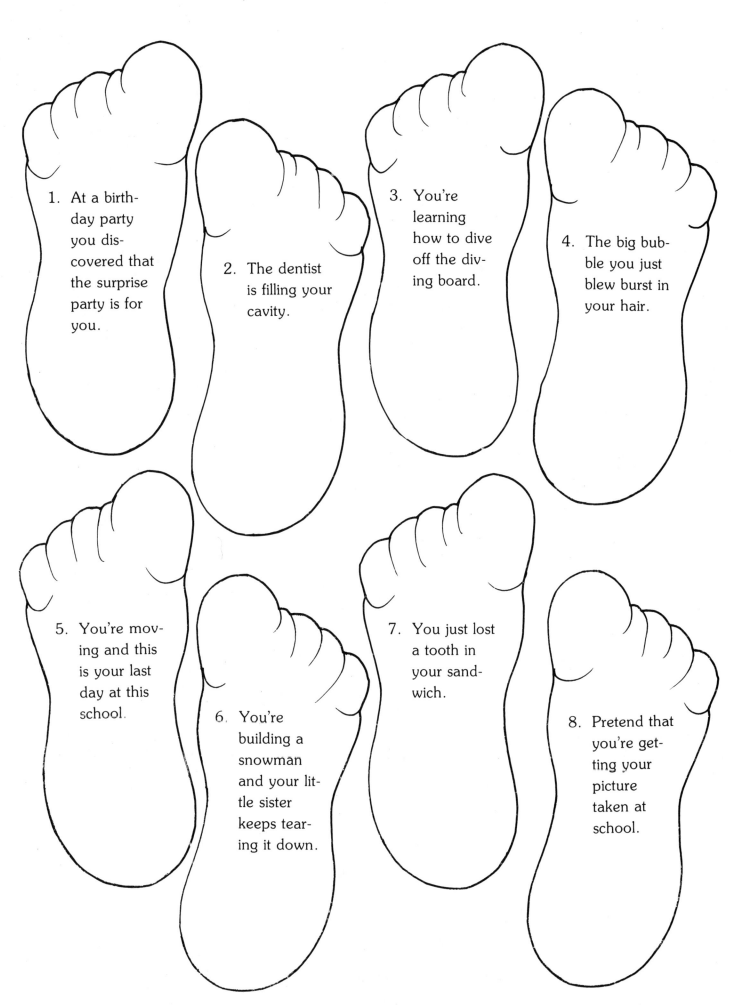

1. At a birthday party you discovered that the surprise party is for you.

2. The dentist is filling your cavity.

3. You're learning how to dive off the diving board.

4. The big bubble you just blew burst in your hair.

5. You're moving and this is your last day at this school.

6. You're building a snowman and your little sister keeps tearing it down.

7. You just lost a tooth in your sandwich.

8. Pretend that you're getting your picture taken at school.

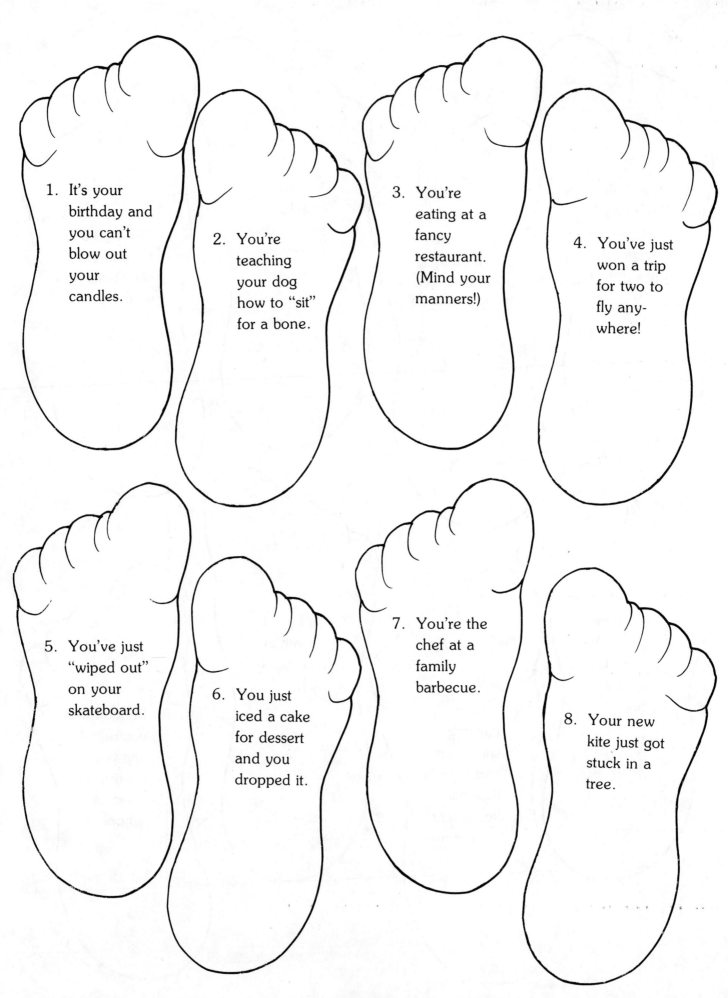

1. It's your birthday and you can't blow out your candles.

2. You're teaching your dog how to "sit" for a bone.

3. You're eating at a fancy restaurant. (Mind your manners!)

4. You've just won a trip for two to fly any-where!

5. You've just "wiped out" on your skateboard.

6. You just iced a cake for dessert and you dropped it.

7. You're the chef at a family barbecue.

8. Your new kite just got stuck in a tree.

TONGUE TWISTERS

A tongue twister is a sentence in which most words begin with a particular letter. Here is an example: Messy Martha made mistakes many mornings in May. Below you will find six letters. Try to write a tongue twister for each letter given. Turn your paper over and try a few twisters of your own.

T _____

O _____

N _____

G _____

U _____

E _____

SOCK IT TO ME

Read each sentence below; then punctuate it correctly.

1. Have you seen my sneakers

2. Our first game is tomorrow night

3. Be a good sport

4. How are you getting to the game

5. What a great game that was

6. Because it is raining, the game is cancelled

7. May I borrow your glove

8. Meet me at the park for football practice

9. Do you know where the coach is

10. Slide

11. Our team won the city championship

12. Would you be on my team

Etonic
Avia
Autry
Spot-Bilt
Reebok
Mitre
Adidas
Brooks
Nike
Foot-Joy
Puma
Pony
Tretorn
Converse
Danskin
Gear
Asahi
Socks
Shoelaces
Insoles

THE SHOE STORE

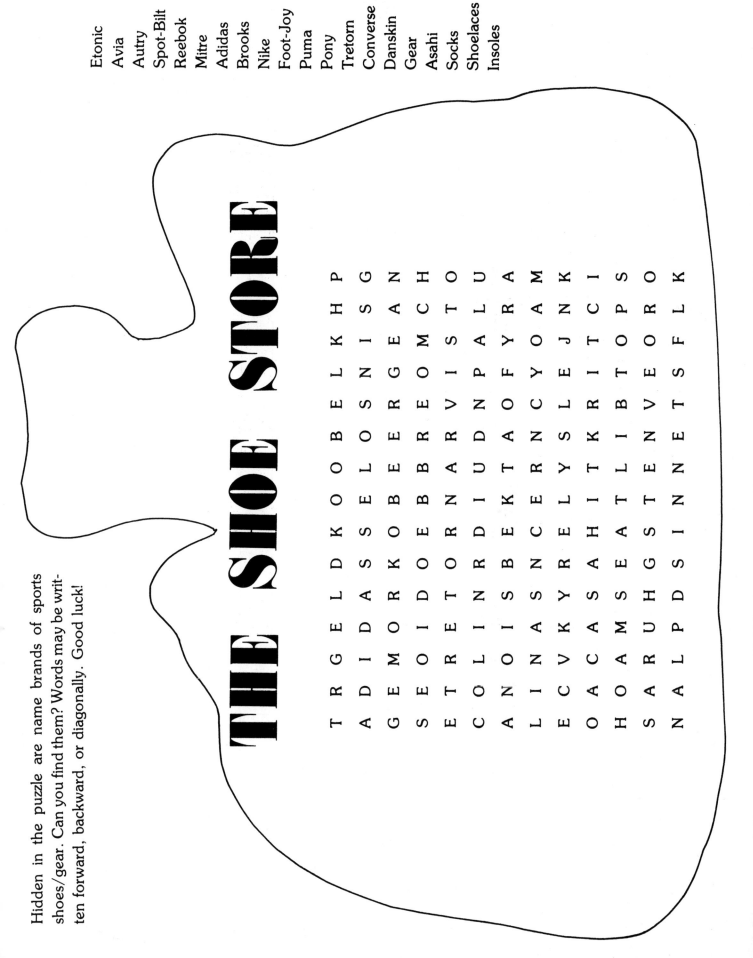

```
T R G E L D K O O B E L K H P
A D I D A S S E L O S N I S G
G E M O R K O B E E R G E A N
S E O I D O E B B R E O M C H
E T R E T O R N A R V I S T O
C O L I N R D I U D N P A L U
A N O I S B E K T A O F Y R A
L I N A S N C E R N C Y O A M
E C V K Y R E L Y S L E J N K
O A C A S A H I T K R I T C I
H O A M S E A T L I B T O P S
S A R U H G S T E N V E O R O
N A L P D S I N N E T S F L K
```

Use the page below for creative writing. Here are some ideas.

1. My Favorite Sport
2. A Real Thriller
3. My Big Toe
4. I'm a "Toe"-rific Kid
5. A Day in the Life of a Shoe

THE BIG FEAT

Carefully complete each problem below. Check your answers. Then try to finish the pattern started at the bottom of the page.

ON YOUR TOES

①
```
   3716
 + 8489
 ------
```

②
```
   8015
 - 1638
 ------
```

③
```
  25,341
 x     6
 -------
```

④
```
 3)7894
```

⑤
```
  79,538
 + 84,497
 --------
```

⑥
```
   6148
 - 4369
 ------
```

⑦
```
  57,918
 x     34
 --------
```

⑧
```
 26)6437
```

121   242   363   ___

115

Story Segments

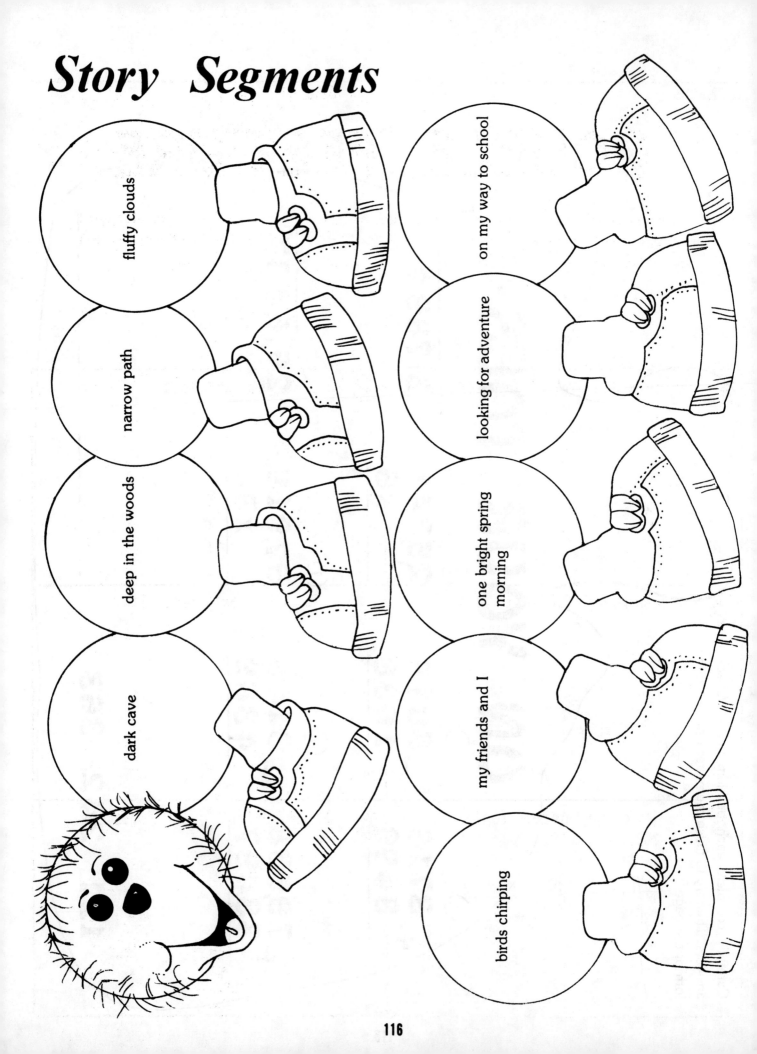

fluffy clouds

on my way to school

narrow path

looking for adventure

deep in the woods

one bright spring morning

dark cave

my friends and I

birds chirping

116

DOUBLE "FEET"URE

Sometimes when we speak or write, we use phrases to make an expression colorful, although it has a different meaning or interpretation. In one space below, draw a picture of the phrase as it is meant literally, and in the other space, draw the actual or intended meaning.

1 To have one's foot in the grave	**2** To be on foot
3 To put your best foot forward	**4** To put your foot down
5 To be under foot	**6** To follow in one's footsteps

DOOR KNOCKER –

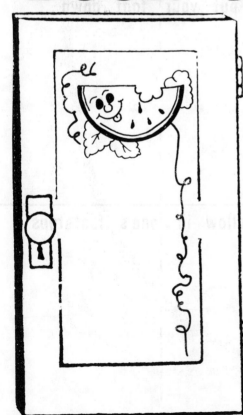

What a delightful way to decorate your classroom door! Title it "A Slice of Summer."

Make a large oaktag pattern of the watermelon above. Color it before it is laminated.

Give each student a ditto of the watermelon pattern found on the next page. After the student colors the pattern and cuts it out, have him complete a creative writing activity. The student's name should be printed on the watermelon slice before it is attached to your classroom door. During the month of May, be sure to feature the creative writing of each student in your class.

A Slice of Summer

COPYCAT

The Sounds of Summer

Splash! goes the water in the swimming pool,
That keeps my friends and I so cool.
Whoosh! goes my little brother down the slide.
Please, please, Mom, just one more ride!
Gurgle! goes the shallow brook on its way—
I put in a stick and it floated away.
Sizzle! goes my hot dog on the barbecue grill,
Cooking supper outside gives me a thrill.
Slurp! goes the watermelon ripe and round.
I spit those tiny seeds all over the ground.
Zip! goes the zipper on my backpack tent.
It'll keep us dry and all the goodies that Mom sent.
ZZZZ! goes the bee buzzing all through the clover;
I must be so careful so that flower I'll step over.
_____?_____ ! goes the cricket as he sings me to sleep
The memories of summer—I'll forever keep!

ANSWER KEY

Bloomingvales, p. 7
Row 1: 10, 21, 24, 0, 15
Row 2: 28, 24, 36, 6, 32
Row 3: 9, 20, 27, 45, 18
Row 4: 35, 16, 18, 25, 0

Rebus Bird Puzzle, p. 26
1. Sunbird
2. Kite
3. Starling
4. Turtledove
5. Umbrella Bird
6. Shearwater
7. Toucan

Bird Brains, p. 33
Eagle = 30
Goose = 61
Robin = 58
Quail = 60
Snipe = 63

Sparrow = 110
Peacock = 54
Bittern = 88
Pelican = 60
Warbler = 79

Turkey = 100
Magpie = 51
Cockoo = 68
Toucan = 74
Parrot = 88

Quack-Ups, p. 50
1. thick stick
2. half laugh
3. sobbin robin
4. wiser visor
5. sour flower
6. best nest
7. rain pane
8. rabbit habit
9. mosquito frito
10. narrow sparrow
11. frog jog
12. bent tent
13. fine pine
14. worm squirm
15. fake snake
I love springtime.

Adverbs, p. 58

Time (Baskets)
1. first
2. later
3. today
4. soon
5. tomorrow
6. now
7. immediately
8. next

Place (Carrots)
1. home
2. down
3. outside
4. somewhere
5. downtown
6. anywhere
7. back
8. upstairs

Manner (Eggs)
1. quickly
2. gladly
3. bravely
4. slowly
5. carefully
6. well
7. softly
8. quietly

Degree (Rabbits)
1. extremely
2. quite
3. very
4. too
5. somewhat
6. completely

Mixed-Up Stories, p. 65
1. One spring morning my best friend and I decided to go hiking. We packed our lunch and set out. After walking for a few hours through the dense woods, we came to a beautiful lake. It was there we discovered the bags of stolen money. Boy, would the police be happy to hear our story!
2. The rain stopped and it looked as though our game would be played as scheduled. I put on my baseball uniform and gulped down supper. I grabbed my hat and glove. When I closed the screen door, there stood Ron. Just as we reached the park, it began to rain again.
3. Last night I decided to stay up and watch TV. Everyone else had gone to bed. I wanted to see a scary movie. I got my snacks and sat down on the sofa, munching on popcorn. Suddenly, someone screamed. My popcorn flew everywhere. I was too scared to move.

Multiple Choice, p. 68
1. B
2. B
3. A
4. C
5. C
6. A
7. B
8. C
9. B
10. C
11. A

A Hare Racing Event, p. 74
States and Capitals

Alabama	Montgomery
Alaska	Juneau
Arizona	Phoenix
Arkansas	Little Rock
California	Sacramento
Colorado	Denver
Connecticut	Hartford
Delaware	Dover
Florida	Tallahassee
Georgia	Atlanta
Hawaii	Honolulu
Idaho	Boise
Illinois	Springfield
Indiana	Indianapolis
Iowa	Des Moines
Kansas	Topeka
Kentucky	Frankfort
Louisiana	Baton Rouge
Maine	Augusta
Maryland	Annapolis
Massachusetts	Boston
Michigan	Lansing
Minnesota	St. Paul
Mississippi	Jackson
Missouri	Jefferson City
Montana	Helena

Nebraska	Lincoln
Nevada	Carson City
New Hampshire	Concord
New Jersey	Trenton
New Mexico	Santa Fe
New York	Albany
North Carolina	Raleigh
North Dakota	Bismark
Ohio	Columbus
Oklahoma	Oklahoma City
Oregon	Salem
Pennsylvania	Harrisburg
Rhode Island	Providence
South Carolina	Columbia
South Dakota	Pierre
Tennessee	Nashville
Texas	Austin
Utah	Salt Lake City
Vermont	Montpelier
Virginia	Richmond
Washington	Olympia
West Virginia	Charleston
Wisconsin	Madison
Wyoming	Cheyenne

Additional Places
Mount Rushmore—South Dakota
Grand Canyon—Arizona
Disneyland—California
Golden Gate Bridge—California
Myrtle Beach—South Carolina
Glacier National Park—Montana
Empire State Building—New York
Mt. McKinley—Alaska
Gateway to the West (Arch)—Missouri
Liberty Bell—Pennsylvania
Alamo—Texas
Cape Cod—Massachusetts
Space Needle—Washington
Superdome—Louisiana
Rose Bowl—California
Orange Bowl—Florida
Sears Tower—Illinois
Wall Street—New York
Green Mountains—Vermont

"Ant"onyms, p. 93
1. late
2. first
3. glad (happy)
4. Many
5. long
6. full
7. All
8. off
9. ran
10. quickly
11. children
12. Boys
13. catch
14. After
15. outside
16. noisiest
17. bought
18. wrong
19. evening (night)
20. dark

1. neat
2. hard
3. ugly
4. new
5. routh

We're Back, p. 95

Nouns
1. May
2. friends
3. hot dogs
4. eyes
5. kids
6. feast
7. ants
8. picnic

Adverbs
1. out
2. slowly
3. there
4. swiftly
5. quickly
6. inside
7. here

Verbs
1. walked
2. smelled
3. found
4. discovered
5. ate
6. noticed
7. marched
8. burrowed

Adjectives
1. one
2. pretty
3. the
4. hungry
5. approaching
6. a
7. an
8. next

Pronouns
1. I
2. them
3. they
4. we
5. us
6. he

Bite into Addition, p. 97
1. 159,112
2. 1410
3. 8437
4. 1488
5. 1699
6. 19,064
7. 16,980
8. 1780

Sock It to Me, p. 112
1. ?
2. .
3. .
4. ?
5. !
6. .
7. ?
8. .
9. ?
10. ! or .
11. !
12. ?

The Shoe Store, p. 113

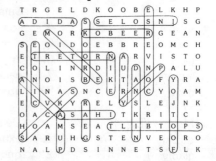

On Your Toes, p. 115
1. 12,205
2. 6377
3. 152,046
4. 2631 R1
5. 168,035
6. 1779
7. 1,969,212
8. 247 R15

Pattern: 484, 605, 726, 847